Unplugged!

Unplugged!

How less is more, chaos is order and grey is the new black
in the quest for happiness and success.

Nicholas Bate

First published in 2007 by
The Infinite Ideas Company Limited
36 St Giles
Oxford, OX1 3LD
United Kingdom
www.infideas.com

A CIP catalogue record for this book is available from the British Library

ISBN 978-1-905940-44-8

Designed and typeset by Touchmedia, Cheltenham
Printed in India

THANKS

Thank you Anne.

For everything. Not least getting *Unplugged!* to the state it needed to be. I love you.

CONTENTS

HAVE YOU EVER?

Have you ever watched a beautiful sunset and realised that everything does make sense after all?

Have you ever enjoyed the simplest of meals — perhaps some grilled meat or fish and some salad — and thought: 'meals should always be like this'?

Have you ever had a straightforward, honest 'no bullshit' discussion with your manager, sorted out some 'stuff' and thought: 'why don't I do this more often?'

Have you ever held your lover in your arms, looked them in the eyes and said 'I love you' and realised there is <u>nothing</u> more important?

Have you ever completed a 'spring clean' or sat down to a freshly tidied desk? And felt great?

Have you ever been in St Mark's Square, Venice very early in the morning before the tourists (even before the pigeons!) and once again fallen in love with the architecture, the stretch of the lagoon and the boldness of the early Venetian settlers?

Have you ever breathed a sigh of relief as the next presenter eschews PowerPoint, projectors, printing white-boards and talks to you 'adult to adult', without 'whoosh'?

Have you ever — perhaps because of a cancelled meeting and non-availability of e-mail — had a spare hour to wander in a city? And enjoyed an unhurried coffee and a decent read of a newspaper article? And wondered why something so ordinary was now so rare for you?

Have you ever heard your favourite music played acoustically – played '*unplugged*' – and renewed your passion for the piece?

Have you ever tried living '*unplugged*'?

Have you ever?

How about if things were a lot simpler, a lot more straightforward again? How about if problems really <u>were</u> opportunities, if out of uncertainty and fear only good could arise? What if learning became your new lust, and you were unstoppable on your chosen path? Unstoppable, and yet at the same time relaxed and cool about what might happen on that very path? How would it be if you knew that things were never, ever going to be the same again? What if tricky became your new easy and grey really was black and white? How about if your mind was an ever more effective resource with access to 'fast-track' abilities such as deep focus and attention, synchronicity and intuition? What if you didn't need willpower or self-discipline because you had incredible passion? What if you were so clear on your direction at every level of your life that time management was not an issue? What if you *really* understood that less is more, that love is the force of the universe, that being what you want to become would enable you to be who you really are. And if you knew what you needed to know even before you needed to know it?

What about?

Hey, read on!

UNPLUGGED: AN INTRODUCTION

We human beings are so clever that we have managed thoroughly to confuse ourselves.

It is well established that we love to grow and to develop; in fact it is vital. The growth process is wired into healthy children (where we call it play) and healthy adults. Without growth, we stultify, we decay and we certainly become unhappy.

A growing human is a happy one. Developing a skill, growing a relationship, learning about oneself, building a team or a business, adventuring (in whatever way) all cause growth and within an overall pattern of basic security, warmth and essential health, an increase in happiness. That's not to say there aren't a few crises along the way; there are, and more about those later. But the general trend is always towards growth.

But we have reached a paradoxical state in our development as a society in the 'well-off west'. Many of us have access to greater opportunities than previous generations and yet we are often less content than ever. In fact for a growing number of people there is a fundamental lack of purpose to it all. What has gone wrong?

We have amazing bodies and in particular amazing sensory input systems. But they do need 'tender loving care' and it doesn't take much for our personal physiological systems to reach their natural threshold, to reach overload and for us to feel 'stressed'. Of course, when we feel stress we rapidly 'lose the plot'. The joy of being alive disappears or is only fleeting.

Many of us are swimming in a sea of data overload, of staggering opportunities, of increasing demands, of 'supersizing' in every sense. Our ability to develop and grow positively has been thwarted. The buzz, the joy, the excitement of being human frequently disappears from our grasp and in order to become 'alive' again, we scarch for the next greater experience. It might be a bigger, better roller-coaster ride, a bigger, better TV screen or might be a bigger, better café latte. It might be a bigger, better house or relationship. Perhaps an even more remote hideaway. But the hunt is on.

So what's the paradox? The paradox is that the more we chase 'bigger and better' for our increasingly elusive true contentment and happiness, the more difficult it becomes to find. The more we chase externally, the less we realise internally.

It simply doesn't work. Like the Man who walks on the Moon and wonders 'what next?', our quest is a fool-hardy one. We have confused happiness with stuff, success with more and love with control.

Ah, all well and good, 'we hear your case', you say. 'We actually empathise with it', you add. But 'what do we do?'

We return to a more fundamental approach, an approach where we re-discover what is truly important to us: we go *unplugged*. Why *unplugged*? Think music. There comes a time when there can be no more added effects to the music nor more electrification. No more light shows. No more bigger orchestral support. To continue to enjoy that music, to remember why we loved it in the first place, to be able to love it again, to understand its message, for the artist to express his/her essential art, we must return to fundamentals: but a particular kind of 'fundamentals' –

fundamentals *which come from having experienced the complexity and sophistication*. A fundamental approach we'll call unplugged. Because then we know we want to be *unplugged* again and we value it. Ready for *unplugged*? Read on.

UNPLUGGED: A PHILOSOPHY

What is *'unplugged'*? *Unplugged* is a philosophy. It is a way of approaching, dealing with and managing this gift of all gifts: Life.

Unplugged does not require complex techniques nor a series of classes; it certainly does not require you to 'drop out' or down-size. *Unplugged* simply requires a subtle shift of thinking, a fresh approach. It is an opportunity to step off the whirlwind ride through the calendar and re-engage with Life.

Unplugged might mean, for example:

- Once again spending time with your <u>real</u> friends in a relaxed unhurried way. Not micro-scheduled. Not 'I'd better go now'. Not conversing solely through hurried text messages nor garbled e-mail. Not needing to be booked weeks in advance. When was the last time you did that?
- Enjoying a walk: almost anywhere. But being unhurried and enjoying that walk: no goal, no thinking 'well at least this makes up for not going to the gym'. Could you do that?
- Planning – in the longer term – to do what you love doing: perhaps, for you, gardening as a business. And your plan coming to fruition. When was the last time you felt that might really happen? That you got way from 'compromise'?
- Once again eating real wholesome food and allowing yourself to appreciate the food, perhaps to prepare it yourself. Not something torn from its wrapping and thrown in the microwave. When was the last time that happened?

- Having some really great time with your son and rebuilding the relationship. Did you ever believe that might occur?
- Once again having some time for you – maybe as you did as a child when time was abundant and available and it didn't need to be 'in your calendar' or 'booked with yourself'. And you don't feel you need to be 'doing' anything. It would be fun, wouldn't it?
- Once again having time with your lover, going to new films, reading your favourite author; and being able to enjoy again those differences between you and him/her rather than resent them. And not even having to justify it by calling it 'quality time'. It could happen, couldn't it?
- Getting post and e-mail which is interesting, not junk. Joy!
- Once again being you, not needing to meet the constant series of expectations of you: no longer pretending. Cool!
- Once again brimming with health and vitality. Being able to invest in yourself.
- No longer feeling guilty about what hasn't 'been achieved'.
- Once again feeling good, positive, relaxed, enjoying life.

The above are not idle whims nor fantasies: they are part of living and being *unplugged*.

THE PRINCIPLES OF LIVING *UNPLUGGED*

When we live and work *unplugged*, we align ourselves to seven key principles, each of which is easily adopted, each of which is only a small shift from most people's current way of thinking. *Unplugged* is a not a 'should' or 'have to' or 'a struggle', it is just a gentle shift of thinking. And consequently of behaving. It is these shifts in our behaviour that influence the results we get.

Unplugged is concerned with the ease, straightforwardness and effortlessness of timeless principles that lie beyond the difficulties, intricacies and convolutedness of much of current everyday life, of 'plugged-in' living. The principles are non-negotiable. We work with them or not: our choice and our consequences. The great artist, the great cook, the great gardener, the great leader, the great parent, the great lover all build their ability, their competence in a similar way: they become more and more skilled, sophisticated and clever until they realise they have been taken away from their core, their foundation, their craft. At that point some chuck it in and try something different. Others, however, realise that to continue to enjoy their work, to return to their core craft, they need to return to their roots, to the basics. But having so much experience these are not crude basics, these are elegant writings, beautiful meals, unconditional loving parenting. Shakespeare performed as it was written to be performed. Each and every one of us displays such a craft. The craft of being a mother, an account manager, an entrepreneur. In our quest to enjoy and develop, we can lose the plot: we make things too dense and problematical.

For example, the chef who has become so sophisticated that he is annoyed that his customers are too ignorant to appreciate his food. Unplugged for him might be to remember that his real skill is one of education, of introducing his clients to great food in lovely surroundings.

The mother who insists her children have a micro-scheduled Easter holiday with commitments for every possible Easter Egg hunt. *Unplugged* might be: remembering what the point of it all is. The point of a holiday? Restore. The point of Easter? Renewal. The point of the eggs? Symbolic.

The Account Manager who writes sophisticated reports about where her time is going. *Unplugged* might be: actually getting out and talking to those customers.

The entrepreneur who keeps thinking up new ways to make money. *Unplugged* might be: simply being creative in his core markets. The money will then appear anyway.

These shifts are small, but cumulatively they create a powerful breakthrough in results; a natural and easy congruence with Life and the way it works. And this is the way it works whether we wish to align with it or not.

Unplugged is returning to what we know when we stop to think: some timeless principles against which we cannot fight.

There are the seven principles of *unplugged* by which we might choose to live. Each principle stands on its own: you can concentrate on one chapter at a time and begin to build the essentials of that principle into your everyday life at work and at home. As you do that you will find that it becomes easier to approach the next principle and begin to make changes in that area as well. In fact, as you will see as you read through the chapters, the principles are also interdependent; linked together in such a way that the mastery of one principle inevitably affects your approach to the next. Once two or more principles are established in your life, they begin to take on a natural directional force that leads you easily towards all the other principles. Used together the seven principles are infinitely more powerful than the application of each one in isolation.

So, to start with, it is fine to work through this book a chapter at a time. But always remember that each principle is linked to each of the others: in the end you will not only need to, but want to, understand the essence of all of them.

You now have a broad understanding of the concept of *unplugged!* We are going to spend more time on each of the seven principles so that you can apply them at work and at home, and encourage your children to adopt these principles should you wish to do so.

UNPLUGGED PRINCIPLE 1:

THE PRINCIPLE OF SIMPLICITY: LESS IS MORE

The Principle of Simplicity: Keep it Simple.

- The essence of the principle: Simplicity is ultimately more powerful than complexity.
- Summary: Simplicity > Complexity.
- Sound-bite: 'Less is more'.

Our working and personal lives have become increasingly complex. We need little reminding that:

- Many of us have to contend with as much new knowledge in a single day as an educated person in the 17th Century would have had to contend with in the whole of their lifetime.
- Most of us have several streams of data input e.g. a land-line phone, paper post, mobile phone, e-mail. And several of these factors are doubled up across the home/work environments.
- We feel increasingly 'on tap', '24 by 7'.
- Add this to the constant barrage of video screens, CNN in the reception areas of our clients, pop-up product information at the supermarket every couple of metres on every aisle.
- The expectations of the family and by the family continue at an ever-accelerating rate: from themed toddler parties with ever-expanding and up-graded party bags to increasingly exotic holiday locations to TVs in every room to...
- We are doing more travelling by road and air, perhaps seduced by bigger and more powerful cars and cheap air fares. But consequently, we spend more time sitting at airports and more time stuck in traffic jams.

- We seem to need more knowledge for day-to-day life: from how to use our mobile phone to the DVD player to remembering all our passwords for our 'on-line' systems.
- Wherever we go the sophistication of technology is exploding and the presence of technology is increasing: the doctor's surgery, the CCTV everywhere, the ever-increasing security demands upon each of us.
- Complexity demands are spiralling. For example: stress is causing us to have more challenges with our health. E-mail causes more e-mail. Ease of access ensures people access us.
- Our brains have little down-time. 'Boredom' is frowned upon. Simply staring out of the window on a train is rare and seen as 'time-wasting'.
- We are increasingly 'controlled' and 'monitored' and must handle growing quantities of documentation.

The reality is that our thinking is now the slowest thing around. We are on the critical path; we are holding things up and we know it.

In addition,

If you work in an office, you will probably:

- Be concerned with regular efforts to strip out cost and maximise shareholder value through downsizing and rightsizing. That will undoubtedly make your job bigger and more complicated.
- Regularly be in meetings which generate actions for follow-through. Your 'to do' list will be ever-increasing in length.
- Feel little stability where you work because of increasing competitive pressure; that will exacerbate the level of anxiety that you feel.

- Have noticed that the high volume of e-mail and increasingly remote management mean that you feel more detached and less part of a team.
- Be commuting further, getting up earlier, getting home later and increasingly accessing remote e-mail '24 by 7'.

If you work for yourself, you will probably:
- Be stretched by increasing competitive pressure, whatever sector you work in.
- Feel inundated by ever-increasing government red tape.
- Find it challenging dealing with staffing issues.
- Be very anxious about your future and that you are not investing in yourself.

If you are a parent, you will probably:
- Feel increasing pressure to ensure your children 'do well' as society constantly raises the expectations.
- Notice that there is more and more stuff that your children need to do, from course work to assessments.
- Notice that you are acting as a taxi service from the moment that your child starts school, or even earlier.
- Have concerns that fundamental values that were implicit to you are not at all clear or being well demonstrated to your children.

<u>Complexity is on the increase and few of us are truly immune.</u>

Simplicity is a way of seeing: for clarity, for what is important. It is a way of hearing: careful listening to the nuances of a conversation. It is a way of feeling: of re-sensitising to what is going on around. Simplicity is a way of doing: 'single-tasking' rather than 'multi-tasking'. Simplicity is a way of responding: how is someone reacting to what you are saying? Simplicity is a way of running your Life. Simplicity is deciding not to be seduced by commercial messaging into buying more stuff which you do not need. Simplicity is restoring an enjoyment for the basics in Life: a walk, a smile a great meal: a ten pound note in your hand which is yours to spend rather than borrowed from the bank. Simplicity is about good design: an easy to understand booking system at work, for example.

Complexity is a way of hiding what is not being addressed. Complexity is a way of building importance and building our ego. Complexity is the way we get confused: an overload of traffic signs, for example. Complexity is trance-inducing: it overworks our brain so that we cannot think any more.

Simplicity is concerned with: what would be the elegant way of doing this? Simplicity is concerned with honesty. It is concerned with vulnerability. It is concerned with authenticity.

Unplugged! is in particular concerned with the simplicity that is the far side of complexity. What do we mean by this? As a human being we desire growth, and with growth often comes complexity: relationships, career, personal finances. The key is to recognise this, to appreciate the benefits that have come from complexity, but now to 'drop back' to managing our life through simplicity. This once again restores your balance and allows you to grow in another area. We are not suggesting no complexity. Complexity is fascinating: it lies 'behind'. The many benefits of the internet come from a huge amount of complexity: but we rarely want to see or experience it; we want a nice simple web-site to use. Einstein's theory of relativity, culminating in the famous equation $E=mc^2$, evolved from years of thinking, blackboards of work. Great relationships evolve from having invested the time.

Nor do we want things to be simplistic: too simple to be of value. No, it is the simplicity, the far side of complexity, we are concerned with. It is this ever-developing cycle: simplistic-complex-simplicity which we wish to ride successfully.

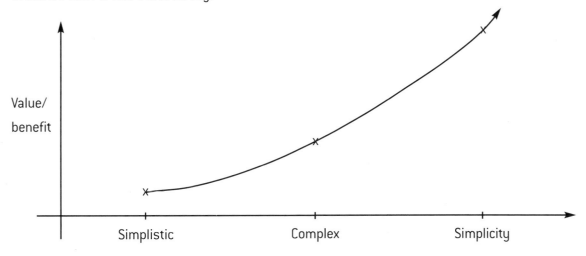

Principle 1 into action. So, how do we put this principle into action?

<u>Firstly, let's understand the factors causing complexity.</u>
Let us just summarise the factors which are most likely to cause complexity and which stop us living this first aspect of an *unplugged* life.

Ten factors causing complexity in peoples' lives

1. **No time for reflection.** Most people have never even stopped to consider this issue of growing complexity in their Life; they have not stopped to consider that instead of adding to their life, if they remove a few things it could give them exactly what they crave. To stop and consider, to regularly 'spring-clean' is such a rare activity for many people. They simply feel that they do not have time to do so. So the bad practices continue. Stopping and thinking is an example of reflective intelligence. This use of 'reflective intelligence' is itself an example of Principle 2 (Mind over Matter) in action.

2. **No experience of living simply.** Many of us have no recollection of any other way of doing things. If we do not know what simplicity is for us, then it is very difficult to create a simple existence. We have new generations who have grown up with TV in every room, with technology crowding their Life, with stress a part of Life. Many of them have never been on a simple camping expedition. They have not been youth-hostelling. They do not know that there is another way.

3. **Ego, fear and lack of authenticity.** These are linked blockers. The first is an ego factor: if you reduce complexity then many feel that it reduces their intrinsic worth. If you are hiding behind a veil of 'busyness', what happens when the veil is removed? The second is a key belief that knowledge is power, and particularly complex knowledge. Remove that and perhaps you lose power. And finally, who am I, if I am not the job title, if I am not the power behind the name?

4. **Data input: screens/games/newspapers/magazines/people.** It is increasingly difficult to hide from the constant bombardment of data; the data flow is greater (consider the number of TV

channels, the thickness of Sunday papers and the number of magazines), more frequent (remember there was a time when news was just 'on the hour', and before that just a couple of times per day) and increasingly continuous. Our brains are regularly in cognitive overload.

5. **'Be' Expectations (personal).** We all want to be happy. We want to be healthy. We want to see a point to it all. And we chase these expectations. When we are not happy we immediately assume something is wrong, that perhaps we are depressed, that perhaps we should be taking some medicine. But perhaps we should just be working with the way we feel, because once we do we will be stronger, fitter and feel more well, in the long term. The conviction that we must always be perfectly well could potentially undermine our enjoyment of simplicity.

6. **'Have' Opportunities: we can – so let's do it/have it. Closely linked with above**. We <u>can</u> get cosmetic surgery. We can travel to the USA for the weekend. And if we see someone else do it/have it, we want it, too. But perhaps we might realise that it is simply not possible. And to chase will spoil our enjoyment of simplicity.

7. **Seduction of the marketers.** We are constantly being sold to, we are constantly being encouraged to buy. As far as the marketers (and we are all a part of that) are concerned, there will never be a stopping point. There will never be enough. There will never according to them be a point at which your Life is simply becoming too complex to enjoy. So you decide. Enough is enough.

8. **Travel 'ease'.** It is easy and relatively cheap to get to Europe, to get to the States. With motorways and trains it is easy to travel the depth and breath of the country. But does that mean you have to? Restore simplicity by reducing your travelling and working smarter.

9. **Technology/equipment/sophistication: beeping.** There are simply too many interferences on our time. How many things in your home and office 'beep' for your attention? Too many, I suspect.

10. **Rate of change.** No sooner have we got to grips with one phone, a new one is out. No sooner do we understand operating system Z than they bring out Y. No sooner have we established one dietary system, it's been discredited. Hardly have we begun using our dishwasher than it seems to be falling apart.

Becoming *unplugged* restores simplicity to our way of doing things. In everything we do, we decide to <u>choose</u> simplicity, to <u>find</u> simplicity, to <u>maintain</u> simplicity. We stop making Life complex. In consequence, we notice that our days become easier, our Life becomes easier, we have more time for our self and for our loved ones, there are fewer hassles, challenges and problems and that things are working for us and with us more of the time. We feel better; we feel we are working in Life's slipstream rather than being buffeted by its undercurrent.

What's it like living by the principles of simplicity? Here are some:

Quick examples

- Rather than filling a shopping basket with food full of additives and surrounded in excess packaging, we shop for food in its simplest state and with minimum wrapping. And if you worry that's idyllic thinking and takes too much time and is even too expensive: keep reading.

- Rather than a sophisticated and increasingly complicated Christmas which in previous years has simply left you exhausted and wondering 'what was that all about?' you talk to all the family about what they want. And what you want. As a result, you decide this year not to travel the length and breath of the country visiting relatives but to set some definite expenditure budgets and decide to have time together. Simple Christmas is born. (Want more on Simple Christmas? – see bonus section, page 117.)

- Rather than two mobile phones, you work out a system by which we can use just one phone but have two ring-tones: one for business and one for personal.

- Rather than buying a second home in Spain and spending a lot of your so-called holiday time worrying about whether the builder is going to turn up and a lot of your non-holiday time worrying about whether you will get enough lets this year, you simply decide to rent a property in Spain when you want it. And you ignore all the 'what you ought to do's' from your friends. After all, the simple purpose was to have fun, not become a property developer.

- Rather than signing up for another credit card because it would help you juggle your money difficulties, you simply decide to sit down with pen and paper and sort them out and make some decisions about how you will get your finances resolved.

- Rather than the three bank accounts which have built up over the years, each of which seemed good at the time, but which now all need their own passwords and sophisticated security systems, you take out some time, close them all down and restart with just one on-line account which suits your purposes once again.

- Rather than having another major row with your lover about the same old issues, you decide to take a walk together and just talk about what is getting at both of you and how you can restore what is fundamental to your relationship.

- Rather than eleven half-finished books by the bedside table, you go through the pile and realise that eight of them you are actually never going to start or complete. You take them to Oxfam. The other three you read on the tube and every opportunity you get.

- Rather than rushing from designer shop to designer shop looking for the perfect present, you simply write a hand-written note saying how much their friendship means to you (and if you're a bloke, you could do that, too!).

- Rather than two wardrobes of clothes, you decide one Sunday afternoon to rationalise and simplify.

- Rather than talking to the team with a lot of marketing speak, you simply explain where things went badly wrong last quarter and how we will improve them next quarter.

- Rather than dosing up with flu stuff, and continuing to work, you simply go to bed, drink plenty of water and get well again.

Note: keeping things simple does not mean they are simplistic, quite the opposite in fact. We'll discuss more later!

Case study 1
Doing a simplicity audit

Richard and Megan have been married for eight years. They have two children, aged four and six, both at first school. Occasionally when they get five minutes together Richard and Megan look back longingly at their earlier Life together, when things seemed so much more straightforward. Now with the children's lives seeming to get busier on a day-by-day basis, Richard commuting and away a lot, Megan's mother increasingly needing daily care, Megan herself trying to run a part-time consultancy, they often wondered what was going wrong ... They decided to do a simplicity audit: to work out what had simply become too complex and needed to be simplified.

Here's what they discovered in their simplicity audit. In the left-hand column they jotted down what seemed to be complex and messy. In the right-hand column they decided to write down what was their 'simple' desire.

Complex: current	*Simple: wish*
1. abrupt 'issue' conversations	1. loving deeper conversations
2. e-mail relationships with friends	2. face to face time with friends
3. endless shopping	3. some shopping, done sensibly
4. taxi service with children	4. less taxi-ing; more autonomy for kids
5. poor understanding of pensions	5. summary of finances
6. health difficulties, stress related e.g. eczema	6. great health

Notes:

1. Richard and Megan's conversations with each other were often not loving or courteous anymore: they were often short, abrupt and shouted across the room or yelled in frustration.

2. Each had friends, especially Megan, but she rarely got to see them properly. Her relationships seemed to increasingly revolve around fragmented e-mail conversations and 'text' bursts. Richard had got into the habit of having a beer with the lads after work on a Friday, but he was becoming increasingly dissatisfied with the repetitive conversations, the noisy pubs, the waste of time. He looked back with nostalgia to the days when he could spend a day hiking or cycling with friends.

3. They both seemed to need to be constantly in Tesco or at their local 8 'til late.

4. Even at this young age, the children seemed to have so many events and clubs which they HAD to go to.

5. The recent news on pensions had caused them to be a little anxious. They were working very hard and they had had a wish to retire at age 50, but increasingly that didn't seem to be a possibility.

6. Where had their health gone? They weren't yet 'old', but equally they never seemed to be fully 'well'.

So, what did they do as a result of their audit?

- They decided that this whole issue was very important to them and they would do something about it.
- When they both got home from work, they would allow each other to 'pour their heart out' into a supportive non-judging environment. Funnily enough, after a few evenings of this, they found that all issues had actually been discussed and they could rapidly move on to more fun stuff.
- Each weekend they would take 30 minutes together to work on things they could simplify. After a few weekends, their Life was really transformed.
- They organised the children's commitments so that one evening a week was spent at home as a family – no car journeys, no friends round. They planned what they would do together: board games, baking, just 'being' together.
- From their discussions they began to understand what was really important for themselves, and for each other. They worked on their diaries so that they each took regular time to spend with friends as well as putting aside time to spend together.

Case study 2
Doing a simplicity audit

Tom's event management company was growing like Topsy with a large number of clients, but ... And there were a lot of buts, such as:

- Few customers came back and offered repeat business although Tom's events were generally rated 'good'.

- Profitability was poor, although cash was always coming in.
- Stress was high because of the long hours Tom and his team were putting in.

His simplicity audit looked like this:

Complex: current	Simple: wish
1. multiple, no return customers	1. fewer, loyal clients
2. chasing £	2. profit established
3. unsure market, goals	3. clear vision
4. stress/let down	4. clearly motivated team

Notes:

1. Tom had lots of customers, but they didn't tend to come back; he rarely got repeat business.

2. He was for ever chasing cash but not making money.

3. He really didn't know what he wanted to do with the company now he had got past the 'start-up' stage.

4. He was stressed.

So, what did he do as a result of his audit?

- Tom got back to basics: he decided he would start working **on** his company again, rather than just **in** his company.

- He dedicated a half-day per month and a half-hour per week to working on the direction his company should take. During this time, instead of worrying about all the urgent jobs that were piling up, he focused on what key actions he should take to move the business forward.

- He deliberately spent more time working on his health so that he was in a better state to make those important decisions and had a better inclination to take action.

- He made sure that he spent time with every member of the company, either individually or in groups, to explain his approach, to encourage, exhort and to praise.

Principle 1 into action. So, how do we put this principle into action?

So what do we do? Take ten simplicity steps.

1. ***Simplicity 1*** Ask: what do you really want with your Life? Ask: what do we <u>really want</u> here? What is most important about my career? What is most important about the children's schooling? What do I personally want for my Life?

This is the 'red light (STOP & think!)' question.

2. ***Simplicity 2*** Decide. Decide to adopt an *unplugged* lifestyle, where simplicity has greater value to you than complexity, from food to relationships. Work on it as a team/family. At your family meeting (see bonus 1), regularly ask how could we make things simpler? Whenever you are about to take something on, consider questions such as:

- *To take this on, what am I going to drop?* E.g. if I sign up at the gym, that's going to mean two evenings per week and much of Sunday morning. What will I drop? Well, certainly I'll drop staying late at the office; that's partly the point of this change. On Sunday morning, I'll replace the time which used to be for reading the newspapers which to be honest are no big deal and I think I'm actually a bit addicted to and I'll be glad to work at that addiction, once and for all.

- *By taking this on how will it makes things simpler overall?* E.g. this new routine will: get me fitter, break the pattern of staying late, break the pattern of being addicted to the newspapers.

This is the 'unplug' action.

3. ***Simplicity 3*** Decide to enjoy fewer things really well rather than try to do a lot of things badly. Films, books, relationships, meals; all become more enjoyable if they are not rushed or fitted in between other activities. Think quantity times quality; keep the quantity to a manageable number and then decide to concentrate on quality. Decide: to focus on quality rather than society's fundamental – mistaken – mantra of 'more'.

This is the 'less is more' action.

4. ***Simplicity 4*** Work at those fewer things so that you move through the simplistic (the 'this is hard, what's the point stage') to the complex ('this is very hard, this requires a lot of attention, this is becoming too much' stage) to simplicity ('this is straightforward, this is a no-brainer. I can do this without thinking about it; truly straightforward.') This is true of the gym, it is true of a relationship … It is true of anything which is worthwhile, in fact.

This is the 'simplicity beyond complexity' action.

5. ***Simplicity 5*** Reduce data input: you can do it. All that stuff filling up your brain. When stuff is filling your brain then you are not able to get the best ideas out. Stop it. Papers, magazines, TV watching hours, Sunday papers. Get serious about data deprivation.

   - Get off mailing lists by returning all junk mail with a request to be taken off the list.
   - Reduce unwanted phone calls: get ex-directory.
   - Reduce junk e-mails and texts: use the blockers which your software provides.
   - Cancel the Sunday papers: go on, you can do it.
   - Switch the TV off: again, you can do it.

This is the 'data deprivation' action.

6. ***Simplicity 6*** Don't try and keep up with the Joneses. Decide now that <u>you</u> will decide your lifestyle and it will be driven primarily by the quality of Life that you are seeking. When you change your lifestyle you will not be affected by what others say or how they think. There are some things which are very important to you and you will do those properly, never minding the comments of others.

This is the 'quality of life' action.

7. **Simplicity 7** Create chunks of time in your diary to do the activities that are important to you: don't micro schedule. Make those chunks sensible lengths. Remember we work best when we get involved in a subject. Too much chopping and changing is debilitating. At work and home for shorter time-scale activities, practise batching them; do half an hour's sorting out the finances and bill paying, for instance.

This is the 'whose life?' question.

8. **Simplicity 8** Decide the ten most important things in your Life now and make them happen: create a simplicity jar, get those smooth rocks and a clear jar. Write on each of those stones with felt pen what is important to you. Remember that if you fill up the jar with the sand and little pebbles of wasteful activity, you will never fit your rocks into the jar. Get them in first, and then see how much room is left.

This is the 'rocks in the jar' action.

9. **Simplicity 9** When purchasing products and committing to services, don't be 'sold-up', don't get stuff that you don't really need. Buy the simplest microwave that'll do the job: don't be feature seduced. Do not even think about buying a fresh pasta-making machine unless authentic Italian cooking is your absolute love. Demand simplicity from your professional advisers. Yes, but what does a 'bond' really mean?

This is the 'low feature' action.

10. ***Simplicity 10*** Simplicity audit. Regularly carry out a simplicity audit. Ask:

    i.   What is bugging me/us?

    ii.   What is taking up unnecessary time?

    iii. What causes the arguments in this household/this business?

    iv. What are the frustrations, the frankly tedious?

    v.   Where do we waste money?

    vi. What things do we do that cause problems down the line?

This is the 'spring clean' question.

In everything we do, we seek simplicity. We avoid making things unnecessarily complex. We realise that simplicity is a very special case beyond complexity.

In essence:
- **Principle 1 is *find, choose and maintain simplicity*.**
- **Move as quickly as you can through the cycle: simplistic-complex-simple.**
- **Key Steps are <u>think</u> simplicity, request simplicity, live and breathe simplicity.**
- **Power Questions; what could I simplify here? Why am I taking this on? If I take THIS on, what do I drop?**
- **Above all, think simple.**

UNPLUGGED PRINCIPLE 2:

THE PRINCIPLE OF WISDOM: MIND OVER MATTER

The Principle of Wisdom: Use your Brain.

- In essence: Mind is ultimately more valuable than Matter.
- Summary: Mind > Matter.
- Sound-bite: 'Invest in knowledge'.

You know that you have an amazing brain; you are often staggered by what it can do, what it can recall, the creative connections it can make. You know what a joy it is when you are able to clearly focus, concentrate well, solve problems and be receptive to new ideas. It's fantastic when you are in the mood for new thinking, stretch and cerebral fun.

Unfortunately, 'brain power', whether it be wisdom or clear analytical thinking or philosophy, is often ridiculed as academic or elitist. Sure, we enjoy the memory expert on TV or the stage hypnotist. But the philosopher who thinks clearly and the leader who wants to reflect before action are often thought of as strange, as are the parents who encourage reading alongside football, computer games or hours in the shopping mall; indeed such parents are often sometimes thought of as 'pushy'. The celebrity status and cult is in. Many people invest more in their car than they do in their brain. You probably don't need reminding that:

- People are reading less (yes, book buying in many sectors is up, but more as a table-top/ bedside acquisition or as a spin-off from a TV programme).
- The art of discussion is being lost. Meetings at work are less about clear thinking but more about who shouts loudest. Families are increasingly too busy to talk.

- People are commonly complaining about the inability to concentrate and focus, and about their constant fatigue. (Family doctors bemoan their patients and 'TATT': tired all-the-time syndrome.)
- School/college and study in general is increasingly about the certificate. An MBA is about the qualification rather than the thinking that should have arisen and developed along the way.

When we are developing our mind:

- We are investing for the future: wisdom and thinking skills tend to develop, accumulate and simply get easier. It is only much later in Life that they can begin to degrade and continuing to use and develop our brains can prevent deterioration in old age.
- The return on investment is terrific. One £10/€15/$20 book can give weeks of brain development.
- Investment appears to lead to an exponential take off in the brain working well.

All work on the mind is an investment.

The difficulty with stuff is that when we are chasing stuff:

- Few possessions, apart from perhaps our house and maybe some antiques, are an investment.
- A fear spiral sets in where we have to keep up with the latest that everybody has.
- For more stuff, we need more money and we are back to the desire for more money.
- We are never content or comfortable: there is always something new to chase or an upgrade to be effected.

- We are being manipulated. Half this stuff we didn't realise we needed until we watched the commercial.
- Investment in stuff becomes a distraction from investing in us; particularly our mind and body. Some will say that they cannot afford to pay the gym membership fee. But they do seem to be able to find the money for a big screen TV. Again.

Principle 2 into action. How do we put this principle into action?

Firstly, understand the factors causing the shift whereby people prefer matter over mind.

Ten factors causing shift of 'matter over mind' in people's lives.

1. **Failure to understand what 'success' really is**. Is it about what you have or is it about who you are? Of course, a bit of both. But where do many currently put their emphasis? For many the quest for success has become strongly associated with acquisition until ironically they discover that apart from a basic level of stuff which they do indeed need, more does not necessarily make them 'happier' and sometimes it can simply make them more miserable.

2. **The mistaken quest for fairness**. This starts at school and leads to a consequent 'dumbing down'. In our mistaken desire to give everybody equal opportunity, we have allowed no one to excel. And if you can't excel you become conditioned to dumb down to the average ability in the class. You adopt a reluctance to stretch and talk about excellence. In short you stop developing your wisdom.

3. **The increasing inability to defer gratification**. We have become a 'quick fix' society, a 'now' society. We appear to have lost the ability to 'hold' on something good for something better. The desire for instant gratification is most easily slaked by a 'thing' or experience. NOW. To develop the mind requires a little more of our time. To be an expert can take ten years! But the journey is tremendous.

4. **Role-models**. The majority of society's popular role models from footballers to rock stars to business people to the catch-all of 'celebrity' are seen to fuel their 'happiness' through stuff. Ironically many of them do learn, and in a big way, the power and value of the mind. Of reflection. Of wisdom. But at that state they have become much more introspective and are not keen to discuss their thinking ... they disappear from view to be replaced by the next celebrity.

5. **Significant messaging from government and marketers** that our worth can only be expressed by our car or whatever ... The message is simple. Get stuff. Be happy. We've never had it so good.

6. **The development of the mind is often seen as elitism**; after all isn't IQ a genetic gift whereas anyone can earn money and consequently get stuff? How often have you heard the phrases 'Clever Dick', 'Smart Alec', 'Know-it-all', used to take a clever child ('too clever by half'?) 'down a peg or two'?

7. **The failure of early education**. Education is something to 'do'. It is of course quite literally the law of the school rather than the law of the farm. Nobody really wants wisdom or learning: what they actually want is the grade or the certificate. To study has lost its meaning. The curriculum increasingly has to be 'relevant'. But what is relevant when we are trying to predict what skill will be needed in a society where the rate of change is vast? If there were an argument to return to the fundamental skills of thinking, reflection, discussion, there can be no better time than now.

8. **Pleasure** has become a function of stuff rather than a function of learning and expertise.

9. **We do of course need stuff**: a bed to sleep on, a kettle … But at what point do we stop? And of course toys are fun. But again, at what point do they become a nuisance and a distraction?

10. **Acquiring stuff is easy; a flash of a credit card**. Developing our mind is seen as hard, especially because of poor associations with school. Developing our mind requires us to sit down and stop, in a fast-paced world where many of us are only able to keep alert by staying on the move.

Becoming *Unplugged*, we shift our emphasis to the development of our brain, our mind, our thinking rather than the accumulation of stuff: of things. We restore the long-term pleasure of becoming wiser, of developing our deeper values, of testing our beliefs, of growing, of considering issues in order to be more effective. We avoid generalising or judging without proper consideration of time or data. We stop acquiring for the sake of acquisition. In consequence we feel freer, we feel lighter. Free of having to 'keep up', free of clutter, free of being compared through the wrong comparisons. In particular we are wary of being seduced by the celebrity and/or consumer society.

What's it like living by this principle? Here are some examples:

- Rather than every evening being a 'telly evening', some evenings are family evenings or 'us' evenings. What do you do? Oh, come on! Read, talk, go for a walk, discuss, go to bed early ...

- Rather than agreeing with our children that 'history is boring', we immediately book a time when we'll take them to our nearest city to some of the great museums ... and re-inspire them with curiosity and the love of learning.

- Rather than giving pride of place to the screen (TV, computer, mobile phone, digital camera ...), we encourage a love of the book; we give our children a specific book allowance. We read to them as young children.

- We couple that with a love of discussion, of expressing and considering different views. (See Bonus section for ideas on family meetings).

- We develop our interest in art and music. We put aside any limiting views we might have about our own abilities. There is a true artist inside all of us: it is simply that some of us have a more popular appeal than others.

- When exercising our body, be it on a walk with the dog or at the gym, we take that time to also exercise our mind.

- We encourage our children to avoid poor language. That is not a request to return to BBC English; language is living after all. No, this is a request to avoid imprecise language. To realise for example the subtle difference between 'I can't' make that phone-call and 'I choose not' to make that call.

- We carry a notebook with us at all times in order to capture our thinking.

- We practise choosing our behaviours rather than simply reacting.

- Rather than being seduced by the 'celebrity' culture and being derogatory about intellectual learning we celebrate it and realise that anyone can develop their mind. Rather than being open to the few, the development of the mind is actually perhaps the one area which is truly open to all.

- We take a delight in expressing ourselves rather than slipping back to the use of a cliché. Be it at home: 'I need closure on this' or at work 'we need to push back the envelope of customer service parameters in this area', we avoid such complete nonsense.

Note 'Use your mind' is not about becoming academic/intellectual in the commonly used derogatory sense. This principle applies just as much to many academics and intellectuals.

Case study 1

Sally worked in a large American bank and she felt very stale. She had a nice flat on a low mortgage from the bank, a reasonable relationship with her boyfriend, but she felt 'dulled'. No one at the bank seemed to be noticing her for promotional opportunities. She and her boyfriend at times just seemed to be flat-sharing. Principle 2 really struck a chord. She decided to give more attention to her mental development: work and raise her standards. She was determined to become more creative and in particular to become more proactive in encouraging her employer to make better use of her. But most of all she wanted to follow her intuitive feeling that she did need to take a new job. Guess what ...?

Stuff/current	Mind/desire
1. Stale job	1. Exciting career
2. Relationship	2. Real relationship. Something more than boyfriend acquisition
3. No interests outside her job. No passions. No hobbies.	3. Rekindled interests

1. It was a job. And that was it. Sure she had taken it initially to clear her student debts. But that was it. Every day the same gossip, the same complaints; and she realised she was in fact a big part of all of it. It was time to step up and move on.

2. The relationship seemed to have come with the job. And it was OK. But there was no way she was going to commit to anything long-term in this relationship. On the other hand she was beginning to build her Life around this person. Time to move on, make a break.

So, what did she do?
1. Ditched the relationship.
2. Asked for a change of position at the bank and got one. A grade senior as well.
3. Booked herself on a martial arts and assertiveness course in order to toughen herself up.
4. Started taking Italian lessons again. Planned to visit Italy.

Case study 2

Susan was very concerned. She was a single parent with a six-year-old daughter. It was very hard because she really wanted to keep the nice flat in the nice area they were in, but it did require her to work hard. She knew in the evenings she was doing work and on e-mail a lot and consequently that her daughter Heather was simply stuck in front of the TV.

Stuff/current	*Mind/future*
1. TV	1. stories/discussion
2. quick foods: poor modelling	2. cooking together

So what did she do?

1. Made some changes in practices at work to bring less work home.
2. Decided not to mix pleasure and work i.e. wine and e-mail. It slowed both!
3. Made an unbreakable commitment to herself, and to her daughter, that the hours between her arrival home and her daughter's bedtime would be work free. She would not answer the phone or look at e-mail. That time was for the two of them.
4. Read a story to her daughter before bedtime every night.
5. Cooked some meals with her daughter a couple of times a week.
6. Taught herself some thinking skills (see bonus section).
7. Arranged a regular 'swap' evening with a friend. One week Heather would sleep over at her friend's house, the next week have her friend over to stay. This way Susan had some regular free time to look forward to.

Secondly, taking action to restore mind over matter.

So, what do we do? Take ten mind-over-matter steps:

1. **Mind 1** Decide to invest in your brain. Switch your emphasis from investment in stuff to investment in brain. Invest at least as much in your brain as you do in your car. At the very least go for 2% of your income. In particular, decide to develop your reflective intelligence, the intelligence which comes from simply stopping and thinking. Use it!

This is the 'invest' action.

2. **Mind 2** Read more. More books and also more widely. Books are unique in that they allow you to pause, consider and reflect. They allow you to engage with the ideas. They offer a far more powerful learning medium than TV. Decide a personal budget on non-fiction books; start with say £10.00 per month. Yes, you can afford it!

This is the 'read' action.

3. **Mind 3** Discuss and talk: over meals or while walking. Practise appreciating other ideas. Different ideas and ideas of people you don't like. Allow ideas to be explored without a definite answer having to be formed. Practise philosophy. Maybe book on a course.

This is the 'discuss' action.

4. **Mind 4** Allow some data deprivation time so that your brain can utilise all of those great ideas.

   By data deprivation we mean:

   i. quiet times: no radio/TV nor music

   ii. no newspaper/reading

   iii. a meditation

   iv. a walk

This is the 'data deprivation' action.

5. **Mind 5** develop your brain (1): Practise giving attention to enable you to get the results that you seek.

   Nothing happens without <u>attention</u>. Family life/business life/personal life tends to move towards complexity because we fail to give attention to a fundamental Law of the Universe and that is that things tend to move to a state of increasing disorder unless we decide to reverse the process: we reverse the process by giving attention.

   Attention is dedicated focus. When we give someone or something attention, it begins to cause change. If we give our garden attention such as doing some weeding, doing some pruning, adjusting the beds a little, it becomes more attractive. If we give our bank account some attention, tracking where the money is going, it rapidly begins to improve. Attention is the primary function of choice. To become more attentive:

   • Look after your state.

   • Practise holding attention on something until it changes as you seek.

   • Practise making a conscious choice rather than simply reacting.

This is the 'give attention' action.

6. **Mind 6** develop your brain (2): practise creativity to enable you to quickly solve problems. By creativity we mean thinking outside the normal standard patterns. Creativity is the recognition of alternative choices. Creativity is breaking a pattern. To become more creative:
   - Practise looking at the problem in alternate ways
   - Develop your creativity tools
     - Think outside the box
     - Break the pattern
     - Realise that the way you are looking at the problem may well <u>be</u> the problem

This is the 'create' action.

7. **Mind 7** develop your brain(3): encourage and use your intuition in order to see connections and possibilities. Realise this is a valid way of looking at things: you do not need to ignore ideas generated in this way simply because it does not seem logical. Intuition is the noticing of what is happening, it is re-sensitising to both what is happening around (for input) and what is happening within you (for guidance). To develop your intuition
   - Slow down so that you are more sensitive.
   - Listen and notice your inner guidance.
   - In particular heart and gut.
   - Consider: 'why have I decided that mind thinking is more valid than heart/gut feeling?'

This is the 'intuit' action.

8. **Mind 8** develop your brain (4): allow synchronicity to become a part of your Life so that the universe supports you a little more and then a lot more. Once flow state is working for us we will begin to notice occurrences of synchronicity. This is where the universe begins to work on our behalf. We tell our partner one evening about an old friend we've long lost contact with, and how much that friendship meant to us – the next day we bump into him in Starbucks. Many people will dismiss this as coincidence. Well maybe it is, but we notice these coincidences, or synchronistic events, because they have some meaning for us. If, instead of ignoring or dismissing them, we pay attention to their meaning and look for what benefits can come out of them, we open ourselves to all sorts of possibilities that otherwise might just pass us by.

This is the 'notice synchronicity' action.

9. **Mind 9** develop your luck by networking and 'right effort'. By networking we mean going out to people, by helping them out so that they are likely to help you out. By 'right effort' we mean considering people as much as the task. Networking is using the power of our thinking to go out and connect with others. Why? For fun, for their development and for our benefit. Networking is just giving a little more focus (see bonus 1) when we meet and work with people. How can we help them? How can they help us? Importantly when we make maximum use of networking we are clear on our personal brand (see bonus 10). Keep your network safe: database or excel or word or a pile of 3 by 5 cards: whatever works for you.

This is the 'develop luck' action.

10. Mind 10 decide to be internally referenced and think for yourself. To do this, establish your values and principles. Then stick to those and decide not to be swayed by the views of others.

This is the 'be self-referenced' action.

Accumulating principles

We are now working in principle 2, but clearly we don't leave behind principle 1. In fact we begin at this point to aggregate, to accumulate the principles. We'll do this with all of the principles from this point onwards.

Mind (Principle 2) + Simplicity (Principle 1)

When we strive for simplicity (Principle 1) in our Life, it frees our mind to achieve a state of clarity which in itself becomes self-fulfilling, i.e. we begin to seek that which supports simplicity. Our brain does not need the external 'buzz' of matter. What we might consider intellectual/deep thinking becomes more straightforward because we are not pulled in other directions. As we deliberately and consciously prefer to develop our mind over pure acquisitive practice this becomes a more regular practice for us and we relish this way of working and we drop too much attention for and distraction by 'stuff'.

In essence

- Principle 2 is 'mind matters'.
- Key Steps are develop, nurture and stretch your brain.
- Power Question: what investment am I currently making in my brain?

UNPLUGGED PRINCIPLE 3:

THE PRINCIPLE OF PASSION: WHATEVER YOU DO, DO IT WITH PASSION

The Principle of Passion: Do it with Passion.

- In essence: Passion is a greater force than obligation.
- Summary: Passion > Obligation.
- Sound-bite: 'Let's do it!'

Increasingly, many of us feel we are doing things because we 'have to'.

- We go to the gym because we 'have to'.
- We read to the kids because we 'have to'.
- We spend the whole of Saturday doing 'chores' – or so it seems – because we 'have to'.
- We spend time with the relatives because we 'have to'.
- We coach our people because we 'have to'.

Don't do it. Decide that when you do something you'll either do it because you want to or you will not do it at all. Do it with passion or forget it. So does this mean that we don't carry out our natural responsibilities? No. It means we carry them out in a different way.

What does it mean to do something with passion?

It means that you look different: there is a new level of energy about you. It means that you sound different: there is something about the way you are speaking. It means that you are a possibility thinker. It means that you are resourceful and energetic. It means that you have an 'I can' attitude. You talk about I/we.

As opposed to doing something with obligation?

You talk about 'they'. Your tonality is low. Your physiology is slumped. Your energy is low.

When you are *unplugged*, passion is your dominant state. For too many people, obligation has become the state. Obligation to play with the children. Obligation to be nice to the customer. How might it be if there were a passion to play with your child, a passion to be nice to the customer?

Let's be clear: passion is a state, a way of thinking. It is not asking you to be over the top in the way you run things, in the way you manage things.

How would it be if passion became your default way to do things? That you didn't have to 'try' or 'force' yourself. It was easy because it was easy.

How about if when you did something and it didn't necessarily seem that initially attractive, you decided to look for the intrinsic worth in it?

Or how about if something seemed almost impossible to resolve, such as you being made redundant and so you 'flip-sided' it? You turned it into something you could work with ...?

Or how about if you realised that your state – as much as what you say – had a huge influence on others?

Principle 3 into action. How do we get this principle to work for us?

Firstly, understand the factors causing shift to obligation.

Ten factors causing shift to obligation rather than passion in people's lives.

1. **'Busyness' and lack of time to enjoy an activity**. Now, we are often so busy that we find it hard to 'notice' what we are doing, to 'engage' with an activity. Yes, we are helping the kids with their homework, but we are actually worrying about our e-mail which we have not checked for the last four hours. Yes, we have taken our partner out for a treat but we are concerned with financial difficulties we have. We are writing a letter to a sick friend, but our mind is also attempting to formulate the shopping list.

2. **Money and status as the primary drivers**. Money and status have become the primary drivers; the standard question is increasingly: what's in it for me? Why should I? We have lost the 'Everest' factor: to do it because it is there.

3. **Desire for certainty and wish to remove fear**. Scientific, modern thinking has implied that we should be able to create certainty in our lives and remove all doubt and fear. We need to remind ourselves that it is simply not possible. And as we shall see in a later principle it is essential for our growth and sanity that our lives are not clinically accurate.

4. **Expectations of what will make us happy/unhappy**. This is not about some naïve positive thinking. How about if it really were possible to view day-to-day activity in a new light and we did not have to focus solely on our two-week blitz in the sun every year?

5. **Non-association of passion with 'work'**. For many, passion is for love, passion is for a rock concert. Passion is even for gardening. But passion 'ain't for work'. But how about if it were?

6. **Messaging: 'the tyranny of work'**. From the earliest age we are told that work will be hard, something we need to put up with. It is rare to hear people who say 'I love my work'. Ironically often our earliest role models, i.e. teachers and lecturers, often show high dissatisfaction with their jobs.

7. **Messaging: life should be easy**. According to whom?

8. **Failure to understand nature/nurture dichotomy**. Many are far too willing to blame genetics and use the excuse 'that is the way I am'. But within that range, we must all remember we still have the ability to develop and grow and become someone who gets even more enjoyment out of things.

9. **Failure to understand that passion is a decision**. In a society where we increasingly expect things to be supplied and done for us, in a society where we are increasingly reluctant to take personal responsibility for our actions and our moods, this concept is fundamental. We cannot choose, predict or manage everything which happens to us. But we can manage our response. Decide to do things with passion.

10. **Failure to realise we do have a choice: in general we do not have to put up with that job**. There are other options. What would happen if we took them? We do not need to accept that poor relationship. At every stage we have a choice. But nobody said they were easy choices.

Becoming *unplugged*, we do things with passion. We have a natural energy and curiosity about what is around us. We stop being unresourceful. In consequence we have a real 'buzz' about what we need to do, there is a huge energy behind us.

What's it like living by this principle? Here are some quick examples:

- We are given the 'bum project' to do at work: the one nobody wants to do. The one with the inadequate budget, the one with the awkward customers. What the heck, we do it with passion! Everyone is stunned. Guess which project we are offered next?
- We work towards following our own personal passion: day-by-day, week-by-week, month-by-month. Through that passion we discover our true craft. Through revealing our true craft we become expert. Through developing an expertise matched to a market requirement we develop a career. And because we are good at it, we earn a good salary.
- Nothing is 'boring'. Everything is fascinating, because we seek the intrinsic worth in everything we do.
- We decide to be interested in and interesting for our children and anyone who is important to us.
- We make that birthday cake/get in the logs for the fire with passion not resentment.
- We are courteous and friendly with people we meet and work with.
- When talking with someone we either listen properly or we explain that it is not possible to give them full attention at this time at this moment.
- We do not have memory difficulties, because things about which we are passionate create a natural 'memorability'.
- We return to things which give us true passion: stories, music, love. We play down false passions: drugs, alcohol, sugar.

Note; passion is not false, 'west-coast' Californian style. It's simply about being your version of being the best that you can be.

Case study 1

Millie was irritated. She had known it was only a matter of time. She'd run a real Italian coffee shop in Harxborough for six years. It had a great atmosphere: early morning for the commuters on the way to the local station; mid morning for the mums and toddlers; lunch-time for business people grabbing quick lunches; midafternoon the school kids. Finally the pre-cinema crowds. Seven am to seven pm was a long day, but overall she had enjoyed it. It did make her a good wage and she loved being part of the community.

But an American coffee bar chain was arriving: big comfy sofas, lovely wall prints. She was really worried. Although her bar was authentically Italian, it looked dated; there were no sofas, she didn't have the range of drinks, especially all the new cold ones.

The first day was awful: the rival bar was packed. Her place was quiet. She felt low and lonely. But mid afternoon one of her long-standing customers came in; said he'd been over to give the new place a try but had left 'cause of the queue and said that nothing would replace her smile. That was it of course: back to her passion. And it was a kick to freshen her place up: fresh paint, more authentic Italian cakes. Twelve months on, both bars co-existed happily. Her turnover and profit were up!

Case study 2

Philip was an experienced trainer who often got fed up with his delegates, his trainees: they were just <u>so thick</u>, some of them! His frustration caused him to get irritated with them. It showed in his voice and in his body language. He began to turn up for courses at the last minute and he stopped preparing so thoroughly. After one particularly disastrous course, lacklustre and boring, the trainees disengaged and unenthusiastic, Philip at last realised that his attitude was making the whole thing worse.

He decided to ignore his ill feelings toward the delegates and just do what he needed to do with passion. The next course he gave it his all. He prepared thoroughly, arrived early having coached himself into a positive and enthusiastic mindset. He made a huge effort to learn names as the delegates entered the room, and used them when asking and responding to questions from the group.

Guess what, the trainees felt valued, responded positively and it was a lot more fun for all.

Level 2: taking action to restore passion over obligation

So, what do we do? Take ten passion steps:

1. **Passion 1** Ensure your fundamental mantra is: whatever you do, do it with passion. Each moment is a choice: choose passion. Even if you find it impossible to feel excited by the task you have set yourself to do, you can act as if you were passionate about it. Maintain a positive body language, use positive rather than negative language to yourself and to others. If a job simply has to be done, you might as well get some enjoyment out of it.

2. **Passion 2** Be here now. Whatever is happening, stay grounded. Be where you are. Be here now.

3. **Passion 3** Be clear on your vision: when you have a clear *want and why* you will find that fear and lethargy are kept in their place. Make that vision absolutely clear, absolutely focused.

4. **Passion 4** Have a fair expectation of Life: no one said it was going to be or was meant to be easy. But Life being hard does not mean it need not be enjoyable. Don't avoid the challenges.

5. **Passion 5** Nurture yourself so that you are brimming with energy: invest in time for you; take sensible exercise, eat good food, take time to relax. See bonus section for advice on MEDS (Meditation, Exercise, Diet and Sleep).

6. **Passion 6** Take care with language such as

   a. I <u>have</u> to do it. Check out why? Why do I have to do it? Ask yourself, what would happen if I didn't do it?

   b. I <u>ought</u> to do it. Check out why? Why ought I to do it? What would happen if I didn't?

   c. I <u>should</u> do it. Check out why? Why should I do it? What would happen if I didn't?

7. **Passion 7** Manage fear and uncertainty: here are three useful mind-sets:

   a. no failure only feedback: whatever happens, decide to learn from it

   b. the past is history; I can design the future; forget the past if it is no longer helpful

   c. uncertainty reveals my greatest opportunities; it has in the past and it will do in the future

8. **Passion 8** Look for the intrinsic worth in whatever you do. Dig deep. What experience will you gain? How will you help someone? There are many occasions when we have to do things which we do not necessarily feel like doing. Perhaps the presentation to the sales force, and we

suspect that they are going to complain about us. Perhaps the children want us to go outside and kick a ball around but we are having a cup of coffee and reading the newspaper and don't really feel like moving.

Look for the intrinsic worth. There always is one. Use your mind skills: see Principle 2.

9. **Passion 9** Flip-side if necessary. There will always be something we can get from any experience. Simply look for the possibility; whatever it might be. To flip-side is to take an alternative view. To flip-side is to change your perception. Flip-siding is particularly helpful in gaining your passion, in restoring your balance, in returning to great state when things are tough.

   To flip-side:
   1. Maintain great state (See bonus section 7, p.123 for help with this).
   2. When things don't go your way, ask:
      - How else might I look at this situation?
      - What good can come from this?
      - What is the universe trying to tell me!?

10. **Passion 10** The quest for happiness does not mean there will not be pain nor anguish on the path. But the pain, the anguish, even the depression is part of the route to long-/longer-term happiness.

Accumulating principles

When we have a level of <u>simplicity</u>, when we have begun to develop our brain, then the two support the easy development of our <u>passion</u>. Passion is our driving force. When we are passionate about something, it becomes straightforward.

1. Look for the intrinsic worth in something.
2. Search for a path of passion.

Passion+Mind+Simplicity

When we work with passion we put our heart and soul into our enterprise, it feeds back to our brain. Our brain works at its best capacity; in particular it allows us to seek the ultimate simplicities which make our life more enjoyable.

Passion supports mind which supports simplicity.

In essence:
- **Principle 3 is *whatever you do, do it with passion. Or pack it in*.**
- **Key Steps are <u>think</u> passion, <u>act</u> passion, <u>live and breathe</u> passion.**
- **Power Question; how could I be more passionate here?**

UNPLUGGED PRINCIPLE 4:

THE PRINCIPLE OF DIRECTION: IT'S NEVER ABOUT TIME, IT'S ABOUT DIRECTION

The Principle of Direction: Choose your direction.
- In essence: choosing our direction, deciding our focus, is more fundamental then attempting to 'manage' time.
- Summary: Direction > Time.
- Sound-bite: 'Take time to plan your journey'.

<u>We don't have enough time: that is a fact</u>. Principle 4 helps us manage this considerable dilemma: so many opportunities, so much to do and yet so little time.

Accept that you <u>don't</u> have enough time. You are intelligent (Principle 2: mind>matter) and enthusiastic (Principle 3: passion> obligation): of course you do not have enough time. Realise that working longer hours, new advanced time management software will not fundamentally help you; they are all 'band-aid' approaches. No, you need to make a fundamental shift in your thinking. And that fundamental shift in thinking is to <u>stop chasing more time</u>, and to *start choosing your direction*, to start getting clear on your *focus of attention*.

Most time management systems only work – at best – for those who are good at time management and at worst cause you to focus on 'ticking stuff off', and addressing the urgent rather than addressing true priorities.

Most time management systems cause you to focus more on doing than thinking or reflecting or even simply being.

Most time management systems are dreadful creators of entropy or, in lay language, further causes of disorder.

However a direction system gets us to:

- focus on what is important.
- notice what will help us tomorrow and long term as well as just today.
- wrestle with what will really make a difference.
- decide what is essential for the long term.
- fathom out what is congruent with who we are and what we need to do.
- minimise stress and entropy.

Recognise that ever since the standardisation of time across this planet (as a result of the need to synchronise railway timetables across the land) 'the clock' has become the measure. The clock and the resulting quality of urgency is seductive. It causes adrenalin to kick in. It is addictive as a drug; we have a love/hate relationship with it.

But urgency does not necessarily mean anything of true importance or anything of a really critical nature is done. And even if it makes us focus on what is important and urgent, we by definition neglect what is not urgent (yet). By focusing more on what is non-urgent or investing we solve our crises long-term.

Direction time is concerned with: 'Where are we headed?' ' What is important here?'

Direction time is concerned with creating systems so that we can concentrate on what is important.

Compare Time management with Direction management

Time Management	*Direction Management*
1. Pull	1. Push
2. History	2. Future
3. Addiction	3. Choice
4. Fear	4. Possibility
5. Pressure/Stress	5. Freedom
6. 'Things to do'	6. Focus Areas
7. Tactics	7. Strategy
8. Management	8. Leadership
9. Lists	9. Projects
10. Part	10. Whole

Notes:

1. Time Management systems are constantly pulling us to do things; they nag us, they cause us to feel guilty. Our driver becomes the desire to tick things off, to reduce the length of our list (which can never happen, of course). They wear us down: they cause frustration and indecision. Direction management systems help us and encourage us. Our driver becomes the progress we are making, which we can clearly see. They excite us about the possibilities which are open to us. We push for what is important.

2. Time Management is concerned more with the results of history, the production of actions as a result of what has happened. On the other hand a direction management system considers the future and what's most important, what is exciting, what could be done. Time management systems tend to keep us stale, keep us in the status quo. Direction Management systems tend to focus on change: what we need to change and how we might achieve that change.

3. Time Management systems often rely on addiction: the constant buzz of another action, the simple pleasure of 'ticking-off' something which has been done, of time running out of the micro-schedule. Constantly reviewing our 'things to do' list. Direction management empowers: the choice of what needs to be done, of what might be done. And we must make that choice.

4. Time Management relies on fear: the deluge of the ever-filling inbox; it is a tidal wave which we must keep at bay or be submerged. At times all we can do is focus on the flotsam that surrounds us. Direction management relies on the excitement of being able to respond to a possibility, of being able to build and address what truly needs to be done.

5. Time Management relies on pressure and stress. Direction Management is dependent upon the concept of furthering one's freedom.

6, 7. Time Management relies on a very tactical perspective: 'TTD' or things to do. Although it is a satisfying approach and one which is very necessary, it can cause the big, key issue to be neglected. Direction Management is concerned with strategic key areas: areas which need regular attention: our markets, our family, our health etc.

8. Time Management is about management: about doing things right. Direction Management is about leadership which is about doing the right things. We can work very hard doing things right. But it is more important to make sure that we are choosing to do the right things.

9. Time Management is lists; lists are fragmented and we lose the big picture very easily. Direction Management is about projects. Projects allow us to see the join and the overlaps. Hence we gain synergy between tasks and the benefits that accrue.

10. Time Management is only ever about a part of the bigger picture. Direction Management is about that bigger picture.

Principle 4 into action; how do we get this principle to work for us?

Firstly, what causes 'time over direction'?

So, what goes wrong? Let's first take a look at what causes the overall choice of Time Management over Direction Management.

Ten Factors causing shift to time over direction.

1. **Time is measurable; direction less so**. Time has become possibly, second only to money, the definitive measurable item. If we can't measure something what worth does it have? Now clearly there are many aspect of Life where the time aspects are critical: trains running on time, the plumber turning up when they promised, our salary being in the bank on the right day. But there are many aspects for which time is not the right question, such as:

    a.   When will you fall in love with me?

    b.   When will I be in the correct career?

    c.   When will my garden be complete and look beautiful?

2. **Time synchronisation is essential in a global economy**. Pre-railways it didn't matter that Bristol and London were in different time zones. Pre the global economy it didn't matter that those in California were just getting going on their business day when you wanted to go to bed. But now it does matter. So time begins to have precedence over the quality or nature of the topic or issue.

3. **The love of data**. Data can now be so rapidly accumulated. Because we can gather data, we tend to do so. But the skill of assessing what the data mean is another issue altogether. And one which stumps many.

4. **Addictiveness of time**. Working against time creates a gentle pressure. That pressure encourages the release of powerful chemicals into our system. It is the flush of those to which we are addicted.

5. **The messaging of doing**. In general the messages from society are to do rather than <u>think</u>, which equates more to time management rather than direction management, rather than thinking in our business lives.

6. **The messaging of achieving**. In general the messages from society are to achieve rather than to reflect. Once again this equates more to the concept of time management than to focus/direction management and valuing being in our personal lives.

7. **Visibility and tick-list of 'TTD' (things to do)**. Although we might buy in to the validity of a focus system or a direction system, the fact remains that the tick-list is straightforward and visible. How on earth do we create valid 'direction management' indicators?

8. **Low feedback for direction**. Either way (effective or not), time management gets you immediate feedback. But for focus, for direction, feedback is slow and delayed.

9. **Status of time**. Time is money. It always has been. Surely all this direction stuff is a bit new-agey?

10. **Those who are successful often quote their success as being 'good time management'**. In fact it is often direction management which has got them to where they are, but the subtle difference has been lost.

Becoming *unplugged*, we accept that we don't have enough time. But we do realise that we can choose our direction, we can choose our focus, we can choose our priorities. We focus on what we are able to do in and with that limited amount of time which we have. We stop clock watching and micro-scheduling. In consequence we reduce the number of crises and emergencies in our Life, we reduce the amount of pressure we feel and stress drops away.

What's it like living by this principle? Here are some quick examples:

• We choose to invest for the future rather than simply raid our resources, whether by raiding our 'cash-cow' customers, or by simply not taking a personal break at lunch time. We invest rather than rob.

- We select our priorities and what is most important to us: we recognise that although we can do anything, we cannot do everything.
- We realise that others have the same bandwidth as us: we must focus on what they are truly going to process rather than what they say they are going to process. We must manage their demands. If others do not live by this principle it is not going to mess us up.
- We question: am I investing, am I utilising?
- We move beyond the demand of what is urgent (the e-mail calling) to what is important (Lego with our daughter).
- We spend some time deciding, knowing and regularly reviewing what is important for us: health, learning, relationships …
- We take some time out to ask; what is my direction? What do I want to address?

<u>Note: direction is not about overly planning or losing spontaneity. It is actually about having more time for what you want.</u>

Case study 1

Victoria so wanted to write a book. She had dreamed about being an author since she had been at school. Although never top of the class or an absolute natural at school, she had won some prizes for her stories and had been very excited when she won a place to read English at Somerville College, Oxford University. Perhaps a little too late it had dawned on her that a desire to be an author did not necessarily correlate with doing an English degree. However, she enjoyed her time at Oxford and came away with a decent degree. She had hoped to have got more writing done during her time at university, but there was so much going on, essays to write, parties to go to, and she was still young; there was plenty of time. She was delighted when she got a job in publishing with a fairly prestigious London firm, but after the excitement of starting work and living in the big city it began to dawn on her that ironically working for a publisher had very little to do with her desire to write: she was simply a 'gofer', she wasn't reading and her 'great novel' was languishing … But she felt she didn't have time.

She needed to get direction.

When Victoria read *JfDI!: Just Do it!* it was a revelation. What on earth had she been waiting for? There was no one! It wasn't a question of time at all. She was the blocker. She was the one who was holding the whole thing up. Once she put the writing of the novel first in her life and began to give it attention there was no stopping her. She began to get up an hour earlier, get to the street where she worked early to beat the traffic, and she could put in an hour and a quarter writing in the local café before she started work every morning.

She made it clear to herself and to her friends that on Wednesday evenings she was simply not available. She got a takeaway supper on the way home from work and spent the whole evening typing and revising her notes.

Now that she had direction, the time came. And it was easy.

Case study 2

Vipul wanted a relationship: a loving one, a caring one with a girl who did want to start a family. But his training as a doctor simply did not allow him the time to develop any kind of decent relationships: the hours were long and relationships were normally quick flings following boozy parties.

He realised he needed to stop and think about what was truly important to him. What did he want? And where could he find that?

He joined a dating agency. At first he was ashamed, he thought his friends might think he was socially inadequate. But at least he was spending his precious spare time in the company of women who at least had some interests in common with him, and who were also interested in a serious relationship. Even if he didn't find his true love, he would at any rate have fun, meet different people and who could tell what might happen?

So, what do we do? Take ten direction over time steps:

1. **Direction 1**: Decide to set your personal direction, to set your personal compass, to ensure you have the focus that you seek.

    Take time to decide what is important to you, and plan to make space in your diary for those projects and activities which will lead directly to your true goals.

    Review your compass once a month and note the actions on your Master List.

For more detailed information on how to set and then implement your personal compass, see the Bonus section and also my book 'Get a Life'.

1. **Direction 2**: Manage each of the six compass points via your Master List.

   A typical 'to do' list is based only on what is urgent, short term and often 'quick-fix'. Ditch the 'to do'; sit and work your compass actions. After a short transition period you will notice that the urgency begins to drop away.

3. **Direction 3**: Create momentum through 'break and date'. The challenge with a master list is that it contains the big stuff, the fundamental stuff. Although exciting, it is often daunting. How on earth do I get this done? How do I break this down? What will make this happen? The answer is to break it down into smaller components and do that again if necessary until it becomes time and brain friendly.

4. **Direction 4**: Create perspective. Take regular breaks to consider your direction. Ten minutes every day to plan your diary, 30 minutes every week to make sure that you know what the important, investing actions are for you that week. Every month put aside an hour to focus on your direction, where you want to go next, how you are doing so far. And twice a year, take half a day as a retreat to assess your life and once again ask the important question; 'What is important to me?'

5. **Direction 5**: Stretch your horizon. What do you want to be doing a week from now? A month? A year? Three years? Five years?

6. **Direction 6**: Read for inspiration which keeps you focused on your direction: 'no one on their deathbed ever said I should have spent more time at the office ...'

7. **Direction 7**: Establish a direction indicator. Draw your vision: stick it above your desk, stick it on the fridge. Look at it every day.

8. **Direction 8**: Ensure you take regular breaks to deliberately break the addictive nature of urgency. Learn how to manage your breathing at times of stress.

9. **Direction 9**: Work on your state so that you have an inclination to act and choose, rather than become addicted to the thrill and/or fear of urgency.

10. **Direction 10**: Decide that you will start following your direction now.

Accumulating principles

With simplicity and mind development creating passion we have direction. With direction, what is important does become done. We no longer get lost in what is less important.

Direction + Passion + Mind + Simple

Choosing our direction conserves our energy, enabling us to have passion for what is important, choosing our direction allows us to put aside stress ...

When we work with passion we put our heart and soul into our enterprise, it feeds back to our brain. Our brain works at its best capacity; in particular it allows us to seek the ultimate simplicities which make our life more enjoyable.

Direction supports passion which supports mind which supports simplicity.

In essence:

- **Principle 4 is *choose your direction*.**
- **Key Steps are <u>think</u> direction rather than time, <u>important</u> rather than urgent, investment rather than exploit.**
- **Power Question; what am I chasing here?**

UNPLUGGED PRINCIPLE 5:

THE PRINCIPLE OF POSSIBILITY: THINK OUTSIDE THE BOX

The Principle of Possibility: Accept uncertainty, accept chaos: manage possibility.

- In essence: Chaos, uncertainty, is as valuable as order.
- Summary: Chaos > Order.
- Sound-bite: 'Grey is the new Black'.

But first, some help with these terms:

Complicated system	*Chaotic system*	*Messy system*
1. The London Underground	1. The weather	1. Dirt on the street
2. How pensions work	2. Career decisions	2. No pension plan

A complicated system is a process or system which makes demands of our brain to fully understand it. It is often dependent upon some talent in the field. Simple strategies can be originated which are fully reliable e.g. calculus, pension tables. Apart from possible intelligence limits, it is possible to fully understand these systems and, apart from 'acts of God', to predict what will happen.

A chaotic system is one that is difficult to understand, difficult to get the human head around. It often requires considerable expertise or time spent in that field and patience to fully understand it. Some simple strategies can eventually be concluded but these are never fully reliable. E.g. the weather, human relationships, the stock market.

A messy system is one which is not given attention. There are therefore no discernable patterns apart from the one of the system getting more messy. E.g. an overgrown garden.

Let's look at this business of chaos from two perspectives. The first is that the potential for chaos in our Lives is undoubtedly increasing because of the complexity, speed and interdependencies we are introducing to our lives. All of these add nodes to the network. What network? The network of action and reaction; I make a phone call, what is the consequence? I order a book on Amazon, what is the consequence? All of these increase the fuel of entropy. This chaos does need to be managed otherwise it literally becomes unbearable for the human brain.

The second is that on the other hand, great things can come out of a chaotic system:
• A spring day out of the storm.
• A deeper love out of the argument.
• Discovering a fascinating CD while getting 'lost' in the bowels of Amazon's music section.

We can miss out on the grandeur, the magic of life if we insist on absolute order.

The careful juxtaposition of the two ways of looking at chaos is itself a chaotic system which requires our patience and practice.

In our day-to-day lives we notice that disorder and chaos is the norm:

• We forget one piece of shopping and the dinner party could be significantly affected.
• One set of traffic lights goes down and the city is gridlocked.
• One small thing seems to set our relationship back significantly.

And that has always been the case. Inter-dependencies often have huge implications which are far-reaching. However we now have an extra challenge in that four factors have made this process even more tricky to manage:

1. Speed. Everything is now faster; the speed of data transfer, the speed of 'new' news, the speed of travel.

2. Reach. Everything is now within an easier reach. Information via the internet. Destinations on the globe.

3. Data volume. There is so much available to us at surprisingly fine levels of detail.

4. Expectations. These continue to rise. Expectations of an ordered life. Expectations of predictability. Expectations of a career path.

And this process will only continue. Here is not the place to debate the point of no return, the so-called 'singularity event'. Let it simply be stated that we are living in a time when the critical path of thinking is slipping away from the human to the machine if we insist on not embracing another way of thinking: possibility thinking.

Because in order to manage this process, this 'confusion' and 'chaos', we try and control it and/or we retry and predict it or we even try and avoid it. Whatever, we must realise that a fundamental part of *unplugged* is realising that we cannot control all that is around us. We cannot predict all that is around us.

Take the weather

Control. We want to control the weather. We attempt to put a % to the chance of rain. What does it mean, 'a 24% chance of rain'?

In countries such as the UK with very variable climates we still desperately hang on to the forecast, knowing they rarely work or rarely work accurately enough.

We cannot control the weather; but we can begin to notice some patterns.

Take a relationship

Control. We want to control our partner. They 'should' be happy at the right time. They should be concerned when we are concerned, interested when we are interested. They can't be: they are remarkably complex. Couple that with the interaction with you and they are even more (not even double, perhaps squared!) complicated.

We cannot control a relationship, but we can begin to notice some patterns.

Take another nation

Control. We wish them to adopt our culture. They 'ought' to appreciate our way of doing things. No. Maybe there are some things they can learn from us. But there will no doubt be a lot we can learn from them. Who wants a homogenous world anyway? We want a peaceful world; but that is more likely to come from a well-managed heterogeneous world than a forced homogenous world.

It cannot be done.

There are two factors at play:

1. Our lives are more complex so more chaos is exposed.

2. The rate of change is increasing, so that we don't have a chance to spot the underlying patterns to help us manage.

Perhaps once, the number of people we knew, the number of relationships we had, the tasks we needed to undertake were all of a manageable proportion. Now, however, with demanding organisations, with ease of communication, the number of 'nodes' on our network is ever increasing. Each and every day every one of us is dealing with a myriad of complex chaotic systems. Our personal systems are not able to control them: we need a new way of working. A new way of thinking.

The seven principles of *unplugged* are themselves a chaotic system; how can we on the one hand crave simplicity and on the other respect chaotic systems? <u>By respecting and working with chaos and uncertainty we rediscover simplicity.</u>

Firstly, let's understand ten factors which cause a quest for order over chaos.

1. **Order is the 'modern/western' model.** From the earliest time we are encouraged to seek predictability and order. It wasn't so long ago that babies were encouraged to sleep at particular times 'to get them into a routine', that bottle feeding was seen as more 'modern'. We have – in general, anyway – realised we perhaps went a little too far with that approach. And we are not saying we should ignore or dispel routine. Children do like to know where they stand: that is simplicity, that is love. But if their artwork, if their writing, even their evening meal is overly formalised how can we get them to grow?

2. **Order is measurable**. Order is measurable. We try and we try to measure the weather. We try and we try to answer the question 'how much does she love me?' Increasing amounts of data from increasing numbers of perspectives and angles; but it doesn't seem to help. The data can continue to miss the point.

3. **Order holds no fear**. Chaos is unsettling. What will happen next? How will I cope with this round of down-sizing? 'I love my routine.'

4. **Order is scientific**. And therefore it must be right! Whether it is Darwinian evolutionists suggesting there is no room for god in their model to doctors having no truck with 'complementary medicine', such polarised views never help the debate and allow us to see the real opportunities beyond such argument.

5. **Order is controlling**. And therefore it must be helpful! When we can measure people it is easier to control them. The average number of sales calls you make per day. The average cost per training day has been reduced by 12% over the last 18 months. Such data is meaningless without the bigger context. Are the sales calls any good? Are the training courses getting the results that we seek?

6. **Newtonian/Cartesian thinking**. 'If-then' thinking encourages us to believe that we can predict and control, that things are black and white. But we know they are not. Light is neither particle nor wave. It's actually both. People are neither controlled nor emotional: they are both.

7. **Man has to be able to manage nature (the alternative is very primitive)**. If we cannot predict, what does that say about our place in the universe? What does it say about the role of science?

8. **Order is reproducible**. Order, by definition, is reproducible. That makes it very easy to work with. August was sunny in Normandy last year so let us go for our holiday in the same two weeks.

9. **Order is easily improved**. Order, by definition, stays and therefore it is easy to build upon it, step by step: that is of course very attractive.

10. **Order management requires less skill and exposure**. And that is cheaper and easier. To manage chaos and uncertainty and notice the underlying patterns requires a deeper level of thinking in which too many of us have had insufficient practice.

Becoming *unplugged*, we accept that much of our day-to-day living is potentially thwarted by an increase in entropy, an increase in chaos, an increase in uncertainty. We decide to work with it and live with a certain degree of uncertainty and a flexible amount of security. We stop expecting certainty and trying to control all that is around us and trying to predict everything that is happening. We realise that for the freedom we desire we must let go of full security.

What's it like living by this principle? Here are some quick examples:

- We accept we cannot fully plan for the weather; so there is no point letting it ruin our day.
- Once we have internalised that, we realise that weather is a chaotic system and much of life is like that: we cannot plan for everything in our life; so don't let chaos ruin your Life.

- We note the beauty of chaotic systems, that interesting opportunities or possibilities arise and develop for us.
- Our being made redundant, the book being rejected, our very unpleasant illness: all are examples of uncertainty, of chaotic systems. But all can lead to greater things (a long-term more successful career, a better deal with a new publisher, a different lifestyle).
- We realise that certainty is only a recent viewpoint in human history, in particular encouraged by the success of science and in particular Newton, Darwin and Descartes. And interestingly the great scientists have all at the edges of their subject returned to uncertainty and chaos.

Note: chaos is not mess, poor planning, 'letting it all hang out'. Accepting chaos is recognising that there is a simple system beyond the mess many of us initially see.

Case study 1

Ken and Janey had three teenagers: two daughters and a son. Their first daughter had been a real handful. They had worked hard, however, and eventually established a way of communicating and keeping the relationship loving (see principle 6). But it was hard. Just when they had got something to work; an agreement on only one very late night per week, for instance, another change would be demanded. But they got there. She's now a young adult and mature and balanced and enjoying her first really serious relationship.

But their second daughter: a whole new story! As she hit her teenage years she became anxious and withdrawn. Always hard working and conscientious, her parents began to worry that she was becoming obsessive about her work. She needed encouragement to lighten up, to have fun. She needed permission not to be perfect. A totally different approach was needed. And their son: a third approach, still!

The relationships with and between humans are chaotic: we must explore and look for glimpses of patterns. Be delighted when we find one, but not disappointed when it does not work.

Case study 2

Justin's background was IT. He liked order, he liked structure, he craved plans. When he joined X-soft as a Software Engineer, it was a dream come true: being paid for what he loved to do. Code. Solve technical problems. Learn new complex systems. React.

Because of his success he got promotion to senior Software Engineer, which was even better because he didn't have to do some of the routine 'boring' stuff.

And then he was delighted when he was promoted to Team Leader. Until he realised this was not a job he could plan or control, because people were involved. And they didn't like being treated as simply a 'thing', a resource. They didn't like being 'scheduled' and they told him so. They reminded him that they had hearts and souls and concerns and worries and ...

It drove him spare; how could he create a system to manage them? That had always been his way, even at school, although clearly he hadn't articulated it that way: there'd always been a system. He went on a management course and they suggested regular 1:1s. But people didn't always want to talk during 1:1 s and ...

Justin's introduction to principle 5 made all the difference. He realised the elegance of the thinking: it was after all a kind of system. He was in a chaotic stage at the time and he needed to find the pattern within it.

So, what do we do? Take ten chaos or possibility steps over order steps:

1. **Possibility 1** Pay attention to chaotic systems. Step 1 is to become chaos systems literate. To do this start noticing chaotic systems, start working with them, start using them. Here are some notable chaotic systems which you may not have 'noticed' before:
   - market forces
   - team dynamics
   - your health
   - your career
   - the stock market

apart from of course the weather: perhaps the most famous of chaotic systems.

2. **Possibility 2** Seek the patterns that emerge from such systems; use those as best you can. For example:

- Your local weather. If you give it attention, you will begin to notice patterns: cloud formations, sky colours. None of this will guarantee that you can tell what the weather is going to be like, but it's probably more accurate than the local weather forecast.
- Team dynamics. There's no way you can accurately predict exactly what is going to happen. But with sensitivity, careful observation and attention, you can begin to notice trends.
- Your health. Again, you cannot accurately predict your health. But after a while you notice that your ear is feeling a little hot and this often is followed by a bit of a headache and you notice it seems to be when you eat. A doctor hasn't a clue, but you have created a pattern out of the deep complexity of your health ...

3. **Possibility 3** Be aware that 'easy order' is only a very special case that we happen to find attractive because it allows such predictability. Remember in maths when the stuff you did always turned out to be a 'special case'? Remember in French that the most commonly used verbs are all irregular? Remember in science that atoms are not hard billiard ball like objects? Interesting that, isn't it? Remember that the edge of all subjects is easy, predictable. But the depth, the inside of all subjects is chaotic, mysterious.

4. **Possibility 4** Chaotic systems rather than simple systems will become the new norm. For a variety of reasons but certainly including the fact that we are a small world now, it is likely that chaotic systems will continue to impact on our day-to-day existence.

5. **Possibility 5** Have you noticed how when you have really struggled with something, really worked your way through the mess, the chaos, you arrive at an elegant understanding? That is the definitive, the ultimate intelligence. From such definitive intelligence are derived the true principles of freedom and success.

6. **Possibility 6** Do not attempt to stamp out chaos; work at it step by step, whether it is the challenge of getting fit again, whether it is the challenge of repairing the relationship, try simply to begin the process.

7. **Possibility 7** Finally, for ever more, realise that 'absolutes' do not mean that we have gained security.

8. **Possibility 8** Whatever happens in our quest to become more used to the world of chaos, uncertainty and possibility, remember that there is no failure only feedback.

9. **Possibility 9** Remember that as George Leonard (author of *Mastery*) so elegantly puts it, in our quest to gain mastery we must love the dip, love the plateau.

10. **Possibility 10** Remember that chaos is the new order. Grey is the new black.

Accumulating principles

Once we have direction, we are able to cope with an increasingly chaotic system.

Chaos + Direction + Passion + Mind + Simple

Allowing for chaos, allowing for uncertainty, allowing for possibilities, allow us to select a direction.

Choosing our direction conserves our energy, enabling us to use passion for what is important, choosing our direction allows us to put aside stress …

When we work with passion we put our heart and soul into our enterprise, it feeds back to our brain. Our brain works at its best capacity; in particular it allows us to seek the ultimate simplicities which make our life more enjoyable.

When we strive for simplicity, our mind achieves a state of clarity, which in itself becomes self-sufficient. It does not need the external 'buzz' of matter. What we might consider intellectual/deep thinking becomes more straightforward because we are not pulled in other directions.

As we strive for simplicity, we notice the real patterns that exist; we notice the patterns that exist beyond the apparent hassles of everyday life.

In essence:
- **Principle 5 is *work with* chaos.**
- **Key Steps are <u>expect, anticipate and utilise chaos</u>.**
- **Power Question; what is the pattern in this chaotic system?**

UNPLUGGED PRINCIPLE 6:

THE PRINCIPLE OF LOVE: ALL YOU NEED IS LOVE

2. The Principle of Love: build the relationship, whatever.

- In essence: Love is the fundamental force of nature.
- Summary: Love > control
- Sound-bite: 'do I want to be loving, or do I want to be right?'

Love is the universal force. It is more fundamental than gravity, as imperative as the pull between fundamental particles at atomic level, as universal as oxygen molecules, as awe inspiring as the expansion of our universe. And yet we have a lot less understanding of it and certainly far fewer strategies for managing it, it seems, than either gravity or the pull between quarks. Love is seen for many as merely the province of Mills and Boon novels. Love is an embarrassing word to mention in the business context unless one is working on an ad campaign for Valentine's day. Love is apparently not efficient. Love is apparently time consuming, fickle and certainly not relevant.

Ah, but it is so relevant.

What do we mean by love? Love is a chemical force. Powerful molecules in the air; molecules stirred in the body. But love is also a way of being. Love is a verb. To 'be loving' is to:

- Listen to someone and work to understand and respect their viewpoint.
- Help them to develop to enhance their freedom.
- Support and respect them.

- Allow for their different way of doing things.
- Be there for them, but not hassle, control or 'expect' of them.

Well and good you say for our personal life, but a lot less relevant at work. No, not true. In business, we are simply skirting around the issue. Have you noticed this sequence:

- <u>Serve</u> the customer
- <u>Delight</u> the customer
- <u>Astound</u> the customer
- <u>? Love</u> the customer.

Perhaps not the last stage, yet? Worried about the term? Think about it, there can be no higher accolade. So, why are we so reluctant to use the term? Perhaps for these reasons: we know we're poor at it in our personal lives, so how on earth can we do it in our business lives? It still causes a snigger. There's still an association with sex.

But let's do away with all of that right now. Loving is the way, in both our personal and our business lives.

Compare loving and controlling:

In business

Controlling	Loving
1. One way to do it: 'my way'	1. There are several ways to do it: let's hear yours, too
2. People are the way to do tasks	2. Tasks are just one aspect
3. Stay as you are/become like me	3. Grow and become you
4. Expression is rules/review	4. Expression is trust
5. Result is: adequate performance	5. Result is: highest performance
6. Keeping and confining	6. Freeing, knowing they will return

Controlling at home	Loving at home
1. How we are at 25 defines 35, 45	How we are at 25 is simply the start
2. Freedom reduces	Freedom grows

Principle 6 into action: how do we make this happen?

10 encouragers of control rather than love.

1. **Control 1** Love is so often only seen in its romantic and sexual context. As is often the case in our current society we have lost the breadth and depth to many of the factors in our life. Love, too has become a simplified commodity. There is no depth: we do not recognise the varieties of love from lust to compassion. There is no breadth: we easily ignore the applications of love from healing to influencing.

2. **Control 2** Love is seen as weak. This has always been a particular tendency of the male. After all, being in love causes one to drop one's guard, to expose oneself. As soon as possible many men, uneasy at their perceived vulnerability, try to put up their defences, either through repartee with the lads, or lack of loyalty to their partner. Increasingly we see this from the female. The power of love: regard, respect, sensitivity, helping, supporting, abundance thinking; these are rapidly disappearing in a 'me' environment.

3. **Control 3** Love requires the dropping of guard: the removal of ego, the expression of humility, of admitting mistakes, of going out to people. In a 'me' society this is not easy to do.

4. **Control 4** The media suggests we 'grow out' of love. The popular press follows the love stories of the young, but the disastrous relationships, infidelities, of the older. Funny that, isn't it?

5. **Control 5** Love is apparently 'feminine'; control is apparently 'masculine'. In a society where corporate life is rife, where our rights are important, there is still a move to subsume the 'feminine'.

6. **Control 6** Political correctness has caused difficulties with 'everyday' love such as a hug or a smile or harmless flirting. Obviously this basic concept is as it should be: it could be easy to abuse our relationship with someone especially in a work context. But perhaps we have gone a little too far the other way?

7. **Control 7** Love can be an embarrassing term in mainstream conversation. It is difficult to use it in the commercial context and if it is not used in the commercial context then it is not seen as mainstream.

8. **Control 8** Love requires uncertainty. There are no absolutes with love. We like absolutes. Does he love me or not?

9. **Control 9** A 'contract' of marriage implies no change. And yet of course we will change. We ought to change; but this need not damage the relationship at all. It will probably strengthen it.

10. **Control 10** Society expects us to love <u>one</u>: we consequently don't get much practice at '<u>loving many</u>'.

Becoming *unplugged*, we stop attempting to control the relationship or 'be right'. We realise that there rarely is a 'right' and if there is a 'right' it is to try to understand the other's perspective. We realise that a lot of energy – too much – is put into trying to control in a relationship. Instead we put our energy into working with the person, in working towards them. We resist the temptation to label or judge them. We invest in each and every relationship which we consider is important, for whatever reason. We realise that we cannot stretch ourselves successfully to everybody. We aim to have fewer deep relationships rather than many superficial relationships. In consequence our 'chosen' relationships are easier. We are rarely 'let down' by someone.

What's it like living by this principle? Here are some quick examples:

- Even though our partner is messy, it is only in comparison with us, and we realise that in another context that messiness is their spontaneity which is the reason we fell in love with them. It may be a reason to ask them to tidy up the kitchen after they have finished cooking, please. But it is not a reason for asking them to keep the bathroom like an operating theatre.

- Even though our assistant 'should have' paid in the cheque, we realise they have had as demanding a day as we have.
- Even though the client was difficult in the meeting, we realise we might have helped through a clearer presentation and by asking a few questions about budget earlier on.
- We are loyal to all around us; we never speak negatively about someone who is not present.
- Our children know that we love them, whatever.
- We listen carefully.
- We are careful about generalising about individuals or groups of people.
- We develop our emotional intelligence.
- Our most intimate of relationships ebb and flow. And we would expect that.
- We realise that criticism is simply another viewpoint.
- We return to understanding the depth of the word 'love'. That it is not just sex, it is not just 'touchy-feely'. It is not being soft. It is the definitive force: as ever-present as gravity, as difficult to explain and with fewer laws predicting how it works.

Note: nobody ever said love was soft/easy/sentimental. Love is powerful. When we recognise that we realise that it is the fundamental force with which we must work. Importantly this is not saying that we are tolerant of inappropriate behaviour: whether it be lateness to our meeting or terrorism. We will see how love can be used to work with such inappropriate behaviours.

Case study 1

Simon's reading of *unplugged* was a revelation. But nothing more so than his gaining understanding of principle 6, love > control. He really loved his wife, but he realised the increasing tensions they were suffering were as much about him as what he had blamed on 'her'.

His original view had been that:

He was right. He was doing most of the providing; he was working hard. He wanted to know that certain things were being done. He expected the house to be tidy; he didn't expect to do too much with the kids.

His new view was that:

He only had one perspective on a situation. Of course sometimes one perspective was probably the more helpful one, but that realisation could only come through 'being loving'. Being loving involved listening. It involved empathising. It involved seeing situations from his wife's point of view. Most of all it involved letting go of his emotional investment in 'being right'.

Case study 2

The culture at Grimbles, Harrow & Wollar City Solicitors was awful. Awful? Awful in the sense that it was:

- Low trust
- Low reward
- High punishment.

And that was just internally. As far as dealing with the customer was concerned, the 'olde worlde' charm was merely a cover for billing the client for everything in every way. This had been fine when people had less choice and were more fearful of the professions, but it was obvious now that more and more clients were turning away from the old family firm and going elsewhere.

Of course in such an environment, 'Love' was a dirty word. Love was not measurable; love was an intangible. Slowly but certainly, the accounts were being lost. To cope, their reaction was of course to try to take more control. All that did was cause the best staff to leave and the best clients to take their business elsewhere.

The days of Grimbles, Harrow & Wollar were truly numbered.

10 steps for love rather than control

1. **Love 1** Re-realise that love is the most powerful force in the universe. Love influences people, grows people, kills people, makes people well, makes people sick. Love bonds nations, love bonds people. Love pulls nations apart. Decide to be more aware of how you use love as a force in your Life and in the life of others. Decide to use it as a positive force.

2. **Love 2** Love is a creator, a healer, and a 'happiness instiller'. When we love someone, we influence their, and our, body chemistry for the better. They feel better: they are nurtured. Decide to become a healer.

3. **Love 3** Love is the definitive business force: for the customer, for the individual. When we use love as a force in business, we are talking about the highest level of so-called 'customer service'. When you love your customer you can do no more for them. Sure, they will kick you at times but hang on in there. Just as you would with a personal relationship.

4. **Love 4** Be you. When you are loving, you are clearly able to love yourself. When you are able to love yourself, you are able to be yourself. And when you are able to be yourself you will have no problems loving. And when you have no difficulty loving then you have no problem living.

5. **Love 5** Be honest. When you are truly loving you are being straightforward and honest. Develop the clarity of looking straight in the eyes and talking one to one. Develop the ability to be assertive.

6. **Love 6** Go out to people. Fear has been instilled in people; it is safe to go out to people. You will feel great. Your sensitivity will grow so much that you will recognise the occasions when it is not appropriate to go out fully to some one because they have not fully developed their own emotional maturity. But do remember that by stepping out a bit, you will of course encourage them to grow.

7. **Love 7** Value difference: one of the biggest blockers to love is the ability to accept and not judge. Try putting your energy into that: accepting and non-judging before labelling someone.

8. **Love 8** Love yourself first. Accept all that you are and all that you might become if you give yourself an opportunity.

9. **Love 9** Don't be a super-hero; this is not about losing real human emotions. You will feel anger, resentment, annoyance, despair when trying to be more loving. But that's OK. All of those emotions are there for a reason.

10. **Love 10** Think about:
    - 'Is it better to be loving or to be right?' Anon
    - 'You cannot know someone at the same time in the light of love and the light of justice.' Niels Bohr

Accumulating principles

Once we have direction, we are able to cope with increasing chaotic systems.

Love + Chaos + Direction + Passion + Mind + Simple

Out of working with love comes a whole new inner strength and relationship and team strength, which allow us to maximise the benefits from uncertainty and chaos. Out of chaos and uncertainty evolves our true direction.

Choosing our direction conserves our energy, enabling us to use passion for what is important, choosing our direction allows us to put aside stress ...

When we work with passion we put our heart and soul into our enterprise, it feeds back to our brain. Our brain works at its best capacity; in particular it allows us to seek the ultimate simplicities which make our life more enjoyable.

When we strive for simplicity, our mind achieves a state of clarity which in itself becomes self-sufficient. It does not need the external 'buzz' of matter. What we might consider intellectual/deep thinking becomes more straightforward because we are not pulled in other directions.

As we strive for simplicity, we notice the real patterns that exist; we notice the patterns that exist beyond the apparent hassles of everyday life.

Working with passion and simplicity we notice that the simple most powerful pattern is to do things with love. Love is what it is about.

In essence:

- Principle 6 is *love is an action*.
- Key Steps are <u>accept</u> more, <u>judge</u> less.
- Power Question; how could I be more loving in this situation, in this relationship, with this customer?

UNPLUGGED PRINCIPLE 7:

THE PRINCIPLE OF BEING: TO BE OR NOT TO BE, THAT IS THE <u>ONLY</u> QUESTION

The Principle of Being: Choose to be.

- In essence: Being who you truly are will allow you to become what you want to be.
- Summary: Being > Doing.
- Sound-bite: 'to be or not to be: it is of course THE question'.

One of the particular joys of Life is when we feel that what we are doing is 'us'. Is right with who we are and who we want to become: working towards a purpose about which we are quietly passionate. Perhaps using a skill or talent. Perhaps having a difficult time, but feeling we are making progress. When we wake up in the morning knowing what it is we wish to do, even if on that particular day we wish to actually do nothing. When we find that the threads of our Life are aligned, when we are congruent at every level of our Life.

One of the struggles of everyday Life is when we are pretending: when we are living a lie. Maybe in what we are doing for our career, maybe in how we are running our relationships, maybe in the way we look after ourself ... Maybe in the fact that we are not allowing ourself to be honest about what is going wrong in our Life: but we increasingly realise that there is a lack of congruence between what we say and do and what we believe and are.

What do we mean by this term 'congruence'? Perhaps it is best explained through some examples.

You are not congruent when:

- you lead people and tell them to respect the customer, but you do not respect your own people yourself.
- you are a parent and you lecture your children about drugs and cigarettes but you abuse alcohol yourself.
- you talk a good story in the community meetings but you fiddle your taxes.
- you tell the prospect what he wants to hear rather than what is the important truth.

You are congruent when:

- You lead people and show the behaviour you wish them to demonstrate by living and breathing that behaviour yourself.
- You are a parent and you work at your own 'vices' such as alcohol as well as encouraging the children to manage their own.
- You may not like your taxes but as a citizen you pay them.
- You are honest with the prospect: it's less hassle long-term.

When we are *unplugged*, we return to congruence: we no longer live a lie. Who we are matches up with what we <u>do</u>. What we <u>do</u> matches up with what we <u>get</u>.

Above all, by becoming *unplugged* we will find we no longer need to 'do' anything to make our life real. It will just be so. What on earth does that mean? That we can make no effort? That things will simply materialise? Well, perhaps a little! What this statement means is that by *being the result we seek* we will get a much faster result. Consider these examples:

Example 1

The account manager who acts enthusiastically about his product, but isn't actually enthusiastic. The buyer will pick up these subtle signals. That account manager must either decide to be enthusiastic or find a role where he can be enthusiastic. But why? Because if he is not congruent he will (1) never be truly effective (2) never be fully 'happy' (3) be holding back his/her emotional development and maturity.

He/she must get some support, get some training, get some time out and consider how they really do want to drive their career.

Example 2

A new mother who is increasingly finding it trying looking after her two toddlers. She cannot act caring, she must <u>be</u> caring. Once this overly tired mother starts acting she will (1) stop enjoying her role and start wanting to escape – go back to work for example (2) no longer be a good mother (3) not develop in her other roles.

She must get some time out of the 'doing' so that she can restore her 'being'.

When we 'be' something it's as if we have the correct operating system: it's one which is perfect for us. When we simply 'do' something with no internal supporting system, it's as if we have copied someone's notes: we are as exposed as the naughty school child.

Compare the ways of operating:

Being	Doing
1. Principles	1. Ad-hoc ways of doing things
2. Standards/values	2. No clear reference points
3. Choosing response	3. Hard-wired response
4. Authentic	4. Pretending
5. Congruent	5. Inconsistent
6. Purposeful	6. Uncertain
7. Learning	7. Know it
8. Evolving	8. Static

1. A *being* person has principles i.e. consistent ways of doing things, ways of dealing with an unhelpful person. For instance, knowing how to restore their energy. A *being* person has learnt over time that you cannot argue with these principles: they are timeless and it is best to align with them. Thus an example of a principle might be to treat people as you wish to be treated. A *doing* person works in a much more ad-hoc way. His/her results are thus inconsistent and not easy to reproduce, measure or understand. A being person strives to work within the concepts of the seven principles of unplugged.

2. A *being* person has certain standards to which they refer and aspire. These standards are often values; the values of integrity, of loyalty, for instance. These values are particularly helpful when things are tough, when we face those 'what should I do?' situations. A *doing* person has no such reference points and acts upon a whim.

3. A *being* person is able to, and continues to practise to, choose their response. They have developed the gap between stimulus and response. And in that gap they put some thought, some thinking, as to how they might proceed. A *doing* person acts in a hard-wired way: they respond in the same way every time. Sometimes that response works, often it does not.

4. A *being* person spends time thinking who they are and what they are about. They are on a quest to fully realise and release their potential. They are on a quest to develop their authenticity. A *doing* person pretends, rationalises and justifies their behaviours.

5. A *being* person works in a consistent way which is the same at every level of their Life: they are fundamentally the same person at work, at home, in the office, at the gym. They are happy for people to see who they are in any environment. They are – if caring is important to them – always caring.

6. A *being* person is purposeful. They know what they are about. They have decided their roles in Life and what they are trying to do.

7. A *being* person is always learning. There is no failure: but there is lots of learning and lots of feedback.

8. A *being* person is always evolving: there is regularly a new them.

Decide who you are. Remove the labels that others have given to you and that you have given to yourself.

Principle 7: into action; how do we get this principle to work for us?

Firstly, understanding the factors that cause a focus on doing rather than being:

1. **Doing 1: Messages from school, college, university**. It is a rare education indeed which spends time considering the person and who he/she is rather than what they do or will do (that most irritating of irritating questions we get while a youngster: what are you going to 'do'?). Concepts such as reflection and philosophy have all now been in general neatly manicured from the curriculum, for being too hard, too elitist and too irrelevant.

2. **Doing 2: the 'scientific movement'**. Science insisted that all must be measurable, that if it is not measurable it cannot be valid. If we are to truly work on our being then we must give some considered attention to terms such as mind, soul, spirit. Many of these items are not recognised in the scientific community and certainly get very little mention at school, apart from the occasional Religious Education lesson. This is bizarre: we do after all know what they mean. We talk about 'this team has spirit'. We talk about this organisation having 'no soul'.

3. **Doing 3: the failure of religion**. For so many, religion has not 'delivered'. And with the increasing ignorance in this area, we have failed therefore to produce any kind of deeper level of thinking.

4. **Doing 4: the life unexamined**. Why would anyone want to do that? Not examine their Life that is. We pursue a superficial happiness. No one reminds us that our darkest times might be our greatest times of learning. To examine our relationships and realise that in the several failed ones we are the common factor requires courage. We'd rather not, thank you.

5. **Doing 5: Too busy to be**. We are simply busy surviving. It is a luxury to take time out and when we do we would rather it is not too much like hard work. Watching the sport, down the pub, curling up with a good book. These are all valuable, of course. They are part of fun, being human. But they are even better within the bigger context of 'what is it all about?'

6. **Doing 6: Work systems** increasingly dominate our environment and what we are trying to do. They are beginning to leak into our personal and home environments.

7. **Doing 7: the life of the 'artist' is seen as a special case**. Any artist will very much understand what we are talking about. And many of us will understand if we talk about an artist in these terms. But ourselves? Come on! But of course few of us feel we are worthy of the title 'artist'. And yet, what is an artist? It is simply someone who is <u>struggling to be</u>: the quality of their work will reveal where they are on the path.

Becoming *unplugged* we find we no longer need to 'do' anything to make our life easier. It will just become so; simply by living by these principles. In consequence our Life becomes the one we had always wished for: authentic, exciting, real, passionate, straightforward.

What's it like living by this principle? Here are some quick examples:

• Each day we act in the way of the person *we wish* to become.
• We increasingly know what to do in challenging situations because we have agreed our fundamental values such as loyalty and integrity.

- We develop our spiritual intelligence, i.e. we look beyond the immediate, we notice the consequences, we learn from what happens, we realise there are things we cannot control nor fully understand.
- We act in a more internally-referenced way each day.
- What happens to us each day is great teaching, great training: we decide to learn from it rather than just curse it.

Note: 'being' is not about wandering about in some remote 'Zen-like' state. 'Being' is about engaging that most powerful of software: your brain. Switch it on: at the moment it's perhaps languishing around 2.3 on a scale of 1 to 10 where 10 is fully max.

Case study 1

Leadership did not exist at WizzoSoft. Oh, granted, there were leaders in name. And some very fancy titles, too. It was true also that leaders were paid more than non-leaders, but there was very little leadership going on. So, what was the problem? The problem was *unplugged* principle 7 or rather, the lack of it. Many wanted to be leaders (although to be honest, more for the money than the responsibility). Many knew what to <u>do</u> to be a leader (after all, they had been on the course). No, the real difficulty was that very few wanted to <u>be</u> a leader. Because being a leader meant: taking responsibility, taking ownership, admitting to mistakes, instilling enthusiasm on a wet Monday morning (and for more on leadership see bonus 3).

What were the consequences of this? Well, it was fine when they were a small organisation. Factors such as the pure energy of the place or the rising market or the product uniqueness meant there was genuine enthusiasm among the team. But invariably, these factors erode. And that's when we really need leadership.

Not that it was not recognised. 'We need leadership around here', many would say and then not do anything about it. Leadership courses would be arranged by the few for the many. The few were the ones who critically needed it: they wouldn't go. The many didn't understand the relevance so wouldn't turn up.

WizzoSoft's days were numbered unless they could crack that fundamental aspect: leadership requires the implementation of unplugged principle 7: be>do.

Case study 2

Tom was a bright boy and his love of people and encouragement from those who wanted him to have a 'decent job' sent him in the direction of medicine. It had to be admitted that even for someone as bright as he was getting into the 'right' university was not at all straightforward, but he did it. And university was hard. But he got a decent degree and he ended up as a GP. He was finally there. All the training, but it had been worth it. So what was wrong? He was honest enough to admit it. What was wrong was that there was no contact, no way he could be there for the client. The client was there, but Tom was always at the PC. What on earth was he meant to do? He was forever up against a time slot. He was up against a treatment of the body as if it were merely a thing.

He was frustrated. He felt as if he should pack it all in. But, all that training? It was frightening. Could he really let go of all that investment? As sometimes happens, things occur at the right time. On a plane flight for a weekend break with his girlfriend in Paris he came across an article on Ayurveda. He had of course come across it before, but had to admit that he had dismissed it as a celebrity thing. But – especially for an in-flight magazine – this was a good article. And he was so fired up he spent a lot of the afternoon of their first day in Paris finding a book in English on the subject.

That was it, he knew what he wanted to do, or more importantly who he wanted <u>to be</u>.

That was five years ago, He is now being what he wanted to be. His formal training was not wasted, not at all. He is finding an increasing interest in the subject and beginning to speak at various conferences about the Ayurveda.

See bonus section if you are interested in Ayurveda.

Level 2: How to restore being over doing.

What are the tens step for being rather than doing?

1. **Being 1: who are you?** Take an A4 sheet of paper or decide to put fingers to keyboard. Head the page/screen 'Who am I'...' Below that, number 25 lines. Now write on every line. Start each line with: 'I am...' Keep doing this and keep writing. Do not stop until you get to the bottom of the page. What happened? Who are you? WHO are you? Who ARE you? Who are YOU. Silly? Perhaps. But who are you?

2. **Being 2: start saying 'I can!'** Stop saying 'I can't'. It is true that there are some things that you physically cannot do: don't jump off high buildings and expect to survive. But there are a surprisingly large number of things that you can do: improve your memory, improve your relationships, get a better job, earn more money, solve your health problem. But the first thing you must do is to say 'I can'. Because in this context when you say 'I can't' you mean I choose not to. And do you really? Become an 'I can' person.

3. **Being 3: remove labels**. Do not define yourself by what you do. Nor by your job title nor your age nor sex, nor history. Define yourself by who you are and who <u>you wish to become.</u> You may not yet run your own business, but you are an entrepreneur. You may be 55 but you have the enthusiasm (in some cases more enthusiasm) than a twenty-five year old. Drop the label; emphasise the quality.

4. **Being 4: according to whom?** Take care with should/must/ought. You should? You must? You ought? According to whom? What would happen if you did/didn't? You must go to University! Why? Because everybody else does? You ought to be more political at work. Oh? What will happen if I am not? Language is a programmer of your brain. Check that you use language which will programme it effectively.

5. **Being 5: check your beliefs**. Remind yourself that your mindset drives your behaviour which in turn dictates your actions. If you believe that you can, then you will behave in such a way, and then your results are more likely to be the ones you desire and that will tend to reinforce the belief that you originally had and ... See bonus section for seven empowering beliefs.

6. **Being 6: Get into flow state**. Experience flow state more often: a state in which you simply are who you want to be. You are that writer so your writing happens. You <u>are</u> a carpenter so your woodworking begins to happen. With flow state we withhold judgement of our abilities, we accept our strengths and talents, we get on with it, we have no sense of time. And amazingly we produce, but without overly doing, more by 'being'.

7. **Being 7: Think entrepreneur: build your brand**. What do you stand for? Think of the brands you consider to be great. Now, what about the ones you have little regard for? What's the difference? You've probably mentioned things such as standards, clear leadership etc. So, what are your standards? How do you lead? Do you lead?

    There are brands which excite. There are brands which are dull. Those which excite have spirit, have soul. Decide to build your personal brand to be the latter.

8. **Being 8: Undertake 'being' practice**. Undertake practices which 'restore the spirit', which allow you to be who you are more fully, more regularly, more steadily, more consistently. What are these practices? As simple and as varied as walking the dog, taking a walk, fishing, tai chi, meditation. For more on meditation, see bonus section.

9. **Being 9: Accepting more and judging less**. Practice more acceptance, delivering fewer judgements.

10. **Being 10: Notice connections, consequences and critical path**. Open your eyes, notice what is happening around you. Notice the impact that you have on people. Notice that who you are has a greater impact on people than what you do. Realise that everything you do has a consequence down the line.

Accumulating principles

Being(P7) + Love(P6) + Possibility(P5) + Direction(P4) + Passion(P3) + Mind(P2) + Simple(P1)

When we strive for simplicity, our mind achieves a state of clarity which in itself becomes self-maintaining. It does not need the external 'buzz' of matter. What we might consider intellectual/deep thinking becomes more straightforward because we are not pulled in other directions: we begin to become 'wise'.

Passion allows and encourages us to choose our direction, it conserves our energy, enabling us to have passion for what is most important; choosing our direction allows us to put aside stress.

When our wisdom builds we notice work with passion, we put our heart and soul into our enterprise, it feeds back to our brain. Our brain works at its best capacity; in particular it allows us to seek the ultimate simplicities which make our life more enjoyable.

As we strive for direction, we notice the real patterns that exist; we notice the patterns which exist beyond the apparent hassles of everyday life.

Working with passion and simplicity we notice that the simple most powerful pattern is to do things with love. Love is what it is about.

And when you love, it allows you to be. To be who you really are. To be who you want to become.

Principle 7: in essence:

- Principle 7 is *focus on being; doing will follow; having will result*.

- Key Steps are <u>think</u> belief, <u>act</u> value, <u>notice</u> result.

- Power Questions; who am I? Who do I want to become?

UNPLUGGED: BONUS SECTION

Bonus 1: Family Meeting

A family meeting is an excellent activity at any time, but certainly try and have one formal one, say once per month. How does a family meeting work? At a pre-arranged time – perhaps following a family meal at the weekend – everyone gets together. Decide a rough agenda: what are the issues everyone would like to talk about? E.g. too much noise late at night/not enough notice on school activities/which charity we want to support? An important aspect of the meeting is that everyone is given airtime as to what is bugging them, that everyone's views are listened to. The actions are taken and reviewed at the following month's meeting. The family meeting is also a brilliant forum for deciding what is 'sucking up' our time unnecessarily. See my book *Get a Life* for more information on such work-life balance issues.

Bonus 2: Simple Christmas

Christmas can be such fun, but sometimes... you just wonder... What's the key to getting the balance right? It's keeping it simple. Simple Christmas is:

- Get back to basics: don't be sold up! There are just a few simple things you need. Identify them, have them and no more.
- What's your fundamental goal: spiritual, family, relaxation? Keep coming back to that.
- Ignore the pressures from society. Do you have to have a big party? Must you spend a fortune on presents? Is it vital that the Christmas tree is a work of art?
- Eat some special foods, but not all on one day and all in one meal.
- Simplify the present-giving routine.

Bonus 3: Thinking development

There are five levels to the mental development of our brain.

The first is simply to develop the brain so that it is good at noticing what is important i.e. FOCUS.

The second is to become trusting in our brain, when ideas begin to self-assemble without our needing to do the research which we might normally do as so-called 'desk research'. This is developing our INTUITION.

The third is allowing the brain to break out of its evolutionary encouraged pattern — seeking behaviour to become POSSIBILITY/CREATIVITY i.e. to have the ability to look at problems and issues in different ways.

The fourth is to allow the brain to get 'into the ZONE'. A way of use which seems easy and effortless.

The fifth is when we begin to notice that our brain does not seem to be an isolated part of the universe but, simply through attention, creativity and intuition, events seem to happen at the right time: the process of SYNCHRONICITY

That's *FIPZS*

- **Focus**

  When we choose to give time, energy and mind-set to someone or something, when we decide to **focus** on it, it happens. We decide to chase the girl, we decide to make some money, we decide to write the book ...

- **Intuition**

When we gather sufficient data so that we get a feeling that 'this' is the way to do it ... we simply know that it is. Our intuition has kicked in.

- **Possibility**

When we decide to break the 'default' pattern which comes to mind.

"I'll never start a business like that" ... instead... "what would I need to do to start a business like that?"

- **Zone**

When we feel that we have the wisdom we need, our talent is supporting us, it all appears effortless. We are 'in the zone'. Once we are using intuition we can begin to slip into a flow state. A flow state is a state of high productivity with minimum apparent effort. Develop flow state, get 'in the zone' by:

- Not judging, just doing whilst being.
- Not overly planning.

- **Serendipity/Synchronicity**

When we get extra support, our brain is now so developed that it doesn't just notice some factors, it notices all factors so that we are *pushed* into the right direction/location.

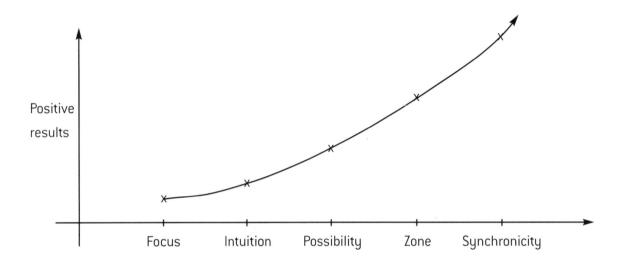

Bonus 4: Developing choice

Choice is an early indicator of the developed mind. No longer are we a programmed, conditioned animal, but we choose. We choose to switch off the TV. We choose to put up with some early battles with the kids over their viewing times.

Choice is fundamental to creativity.

To become more 'choiceful':

• Notice the options.

• Keep the mind open.

• Listen more to the views of others.

Bonus 5: How to do a simple breathing meditation.

To carry out a breathing meditation:

1. Try and do one for ten minutes each morning and each evening each day. The morning meditation complements your sleep and sets you up for the rest of the day. The evening meditation ensures you have a re-vitalised evening and that you sleep well. Try and meditate every day at least once. It is a pro-active mechanism – a bit like brushing your teeth.

2. To actually meditate, sit quietly in a comfortable upright chair. Choose a location which will be quiet and undisturbed, but don't try and find somewhere which is absolutely silent; you probably won't find it, unless you go to a cave in the Himalayas and that's a whole other story! Focus on your breathing and allow your mind to get a little quieter and allow your body to relax. Thoughts <u>will</u> come to mind; return your awareness to your breathing. Don't try and 'not' have thoughts; simply be aware of your breathing (see 5 below).

3. By focusing on your breathing I certainly don't mean forcing your breathing to take on a particular speed or style: don't try and change the speed or to count the breaths, simply be aware of the 'in' breath and the 'out' breath and so on. And if you notice that a thought or a noise distracts you, return to that flow.

4. Some meditations will be very relaxing, some very turbulent. It is often the latter which are the most helpful. Try not to judge the experience you have during meditation, just accept that they are what your mind and body need at that moment.

5. One more time: don't try and 'not have thoughts'. You will have thoughts, don't fight them. Instead, focus on your breathing.

6. Above all, as one of the great meditation teachers said: don't worry about what happens in your meditation – it's what happens outside your meditation which is most important. And as you regularly meditate, you will notice significant change.

7. Once you can, extend your meditation time from 10 to 15 to 20 minutes per session.

Bonus 6: Some questions on personal brand

What do you mean by personal brand?

A personal brand is a more formal encapsulation of who you are and what you stand for in the working environment. A true brand, of course, will be resilient through and through so that it will not change much if at all in the 'non-work' environments. To get a handle on your personal brand try these mini exercises:

• What are your values?
• What is important for you in the working environment?
• If a bumper sticker represented you, what would it say?
• If you were to make an elevator pitch, what would you say?

Is this just unnecessary jargon?

No. It's a useful exercise which few do to formalise what they do and what they are. Yes it is hard. That's the point.

How do I identify, create and maintain my personal brand?

Do the above exercise and then ensure once a quarter you re-run those questions to ensure full integrity of what you are doing.

Bonus 7: Choosing and managing your 'state'

Being in a great state is fundamental to choosing passion over obligation. Manage your state through a four-part strategy called MEDS:

M or meditation

Meditation is any practice which allows the mind to settle down so that we achieve a state of relaxation. The settling down of the mind helps us to experience our essential self without the clutter and chatter of worries and thoughts that usually accompany us in our waking state.

You can learn a meditation technique, either a simple breathing meditation or a silent mantra meditation, or you can use any other technique which you find useful. Many people find that running or walking puts them in a meditative state. For others simply sitting in silence, perhaps in nature or at home on the sofa, can help. What is most important, whatever technique you use, is to practise it regularly, every day if possible. Make sure you give yourself half an hour of 'time out'. (See bonus 5).

E or exercise

Everyone knows that it is important to exercise regularly to keep fit. It is also important to take regular exercise in order to feel alert. Exercise has a huge effect on mental state as well; if you exercise regularly you are less likely to be depressed and more able to shrug off a poor state and access a more positive attitude to life.

Exercise need not necessarily mean going to the gym. It is important to choose a form of exercise that you enjoy, and that you can easily keep up. Start by simply walking more. For instance, choose the stairs, rather than the escalator. Get off the bus one stop early. Walk for a short journey, rather than use the car.

D or diet

We wouldn't put diesel fuel into a car designed for unleaded petrol and expect that car to give us great performance, and yet everyday we fill ourselves with food that we know to be unhealthy and expect our bodies to cope. We're not talking about faddy or weight reducing diets here, but simply about changing our habits to eat more of what we know is good for our bodies, and less of what is clearly bad.

Try reducing fat, sugar, salt, processed foods, alcohol, artificial sweeteners and caffeine. Instead increase your intake of fruit, vegetables, water and 'good' carbohydrates (brown rice, whole wheat etc). You should expect to feel a marked increase in energy almost immediately; the effect it could have on your health in the long term is incalculable.

S or sleep

However often we hear about the great leaders who need only four hours of sleep a night to win wars and run countries, the fact remains that most of us need more sleep than we allow ourselves, in order to function at our best. We also need sleep at regular times. Somehow we wake more refreshed from a night's sleep that started well before midnight, even if we have to get up quite early in the morning, than we do from the lie-in that we allow ourselves until midday on a Sunday. When we wake as late as this we often feel sluggish and exhausted, even though we've been in bed for as many hours as we 'need'.

Rather than trying to catch up on your sleep debt by staying in bed for half of the weekend, try to get to bed early instead, a couple of times during the week.

And of course if you're eating well, and getting plenty of exercise, you should sleep better anyway ...

Bonus 8: Setting and Managing your Personal Compass

We sometimes forget that there are two kinds of time: clock time and compass time. Clock time is the one we tend to be most aware of. A watch or clock is useful for a calibration, a measure, for history, for what has elapsed. A compass is useful for setting direction, for making a choice about 'where to next?' The clock tends to reflect what is important and urgent. When we are working in clock time we tend to feel that we are 'up against it'. We feel adrenaline, we feel buzz, we can also feel stress, we can also feel out of control. We have to manage a certain amount of clock time. The important thing is to manage and reduce it.

Compass time is a slightly different sense of time. Compass time is certainly important. We are addressing our priorities about what is important. Compass time is when we focus on what is important and non-urgent, important and <u>investing</u>. Topics such as health, our pension, maintaining relationships etc. The compass tends to reflect what is important and investing. When we look at our watch or clock, we are working 'in' things. When we consider our compass we are working' on' things.

On your personal compass there are six compass points:

- Career.
- Mind/body.
- Finance.
- Relationships.
- Fun.
- Contribution.

For each, ask a fundamental direction question to ensure you are on track for the Life you desire. For example:

- Career: where do you want your career to be in three years time? How will you get there? Notice the word was 'want'.
- Mind/body: what are three things you could do to look after and invest in your mind/body? Which will you do, when and how?
- Finance: rate your finances from 1 to 10. 1=poor, 10= outstanding. What are three actions that you could take that would improve the calibration? Which will you do? How and when?

- Relationships: which is the relationship which is most important to you? What else could you do to strengthen it? Is there a relationship which needs to be 'sorted'? How will you do that?
- Fun: Are you getting enough? Fun, that is? If not, what would restore fun in your Life?
- Contribution: what are the important 'causes' in your Life? How can you support them?

Bonus 9: Leadership

Note the difference:

'Doing' leadership	'Being' leadership
1. Job title is all	1. Results are all
2. Talk	2. Walk
3. Measure	3. Engage
4. Do as I say	4. Do as I do
5. IQ	5. EQ
6. Things right	6. Right things

Bonus 10: Ayurveda

Ayurveda is a fascinating and exciting personal health strategy. There are many excellent books available, but if you are unsure where to start then get hold of a copy of Deepak Chopra's *Perfect Health*.

Bonus 11: Seven empowering beliefs

Remember our fundamental idea: mindset or belief drives our behaviour. This influences our results. Try living and breathing these seven empowering beliefs. Simply 'act as if':

- I can. Because it's amazing what you physically and mentally can do. 'I can't remember these names' is simply not true. 'I can't get promotion' is not true. <u>I CAN is the fundamental belief of direction</u>.

- No failure only feedback. Things will go wrong, they will not always go to plan. You will be fed up , you may be disappointed. But it is all feedback if you decide to view it as such. <u>NO FAILURE ONLY FEEDBACK is the fundamental belief of learning</u>.

- I make the real world. You do. You can look upon the traffic jam as the worst thing which has happened to you or as an opportunity to slow down for a while and think. <u>I MAKE THE REAL WORLD is the fundamental belief of perception</u>.

- I choose. Whatever happens to you there is the ability to choose your response. If someone is irritating, you don't have to be irritated. <u>I CHOOSE is the fundamental belief of options</u>.

- There's a reason for this happening. A fun belief, but potentially amazingly powerful. When things happen, ask 'what am I meant to be learning here?' What am I meant to be getting from this situation? It could be a person being difficult. Maybe they are telling you that perhaps you could have planned a little more. <u>THERE IS A REASON FOR THIS HAPPENING is the fundamental personal growth belief</u>.

- This says something about me. When things don't go your way ask: what does this say about me? However small your contribution, you will have some. Work on that. <u>This is an amazing belief for personal growth</u>.

- There's always a way. <u>There is. Go for it!</u>

LIVING *UNPLUGGED*: LIVE AND BREATHE

You now have a very good understanding of *Unplugged*. Having read this far you will no doubt already be adopting some of the principles into your daily Life: excellent. This section is simply to help you accelerate that process and progress. We'll firstly look at some general principles of getting change to happen and then some specifics for 'wiring it in' to your daily activity.

Firstly, some general points:

<u>Work on one principle at a time.</u>
Keep it simple! It's initially exciting to be attempting to walk and talk all of the principles, but perhaps you will lose momentum. Just take one principle – any one – and 'work it' until you find you no longer need to give it attention – you find that you are just using it. You'll probably find you'll go through the four classic stages of learning:

- Unconscious incompetence: low awareness of what is needed (if you're a car driver you'll remember those first few lessons: you hadn't realised there was so much to it).
- Conscious incompetence: aware of the changes that are required (continuing the analogy, you now know what a poor driver you were).

- Conscious competence: the changes are being implemented, but need effort (now you're not bad at all, but you do need to concentrate on the skills).
- Unconscious competence: the changes are wired in and rarely need conscious effort, you are 'living and breathing' the changes (and now a fantastic stage: you can do it and it's 'easy').

Look for opportunities to use the principles

The sense of frustration is one which clearly signals that something is wrong. When you feel it, see which of the seven principles of *unplugged* is most likely to help: there is always one which will.

Try and work with a buddy

It can be tough doing all this stuff on your own at times. Find a buddy! There is someone out there who wants to work on these ideas with you. You may be very fortunate and it is your partner (life or business), but if not strive to find someone. They don't need to have any apparent challenges or perhaps they do: depression, a difficult relationship, coping with the loss of a job. But they must be keen; if you have to bully them into it it's just going to be one more thing for you to be concerned about. And what do you do? How do you get this thing to work? Cajole each other to work on the principles. Explain to each other your understanding of the concepts. Get together formally occasionally and review progress and, most importantly, when one is feeling down or is beginning to lose the plot, get them back on the path.

Do not beat yourself up: keep trying. Persist and get feedback.

Personal change is not on/off, it's more a sliding scale. It is a bit of progress (often dramatic), a set back or two. A bit more progress. A disaster followed by a real breakthrough etc. Just hang on in there. Above all remember that when you feel you have 'failed' you have simply got some feedback, and that the number one characteristic in getting these ideas to work for you is persistence.

<u>Incorporate it into all parts of your Life</u>
And that's what we are particularly going to look at now. Most importantly don't just keep this for 'home' or family Life. Make it run through all of your Life.

LIVING *UNPLUGGED*: AT WORK

Use the following framework to restore, reinforce and accelerate your '*unplugged*' approach at your place of work. Take a piece of paper or put fingers to keyboard and answer each of these questions as quickly and as honestly as you can. It is important that you write quickly and do not dwell too long trying to be 'correct'.

Please start:

Unplugged Principle 1: the principle of simplicity

- What is the purpose of your job? What do you deliver? <u>Write it down</u>.
- What stops and/or blocks you from being able to give your purpose 100% attention? <u>Write it down</u>.
- What are your distracters? <u>Write them down</u>.
- Who are your distracters? <u>Write them down</u>.
- If your job were restored to its very essence, what would it be? <u>Write it down</u>.
- Write a bumper sticker for your job! <u>Do it now</u>.
- If you had the luxury of a full-time assistant, what would you delegate to him or her? <u>Write it down</u>.

Now, pause for a few minutes. Read all of your answers. Again, put pen to paper or fingers to keyboard and write as quickly as you can the continuation to this statement:

I can restore simplicity to my work by carrying out the following three highest pay-off actions:

1. _____

2. _____

3. _____

<u>Example</u>

I can restore simplicity to my work by carrying out the following three actions:

1. I will have a detailed discussion with my boss about what my job is all about. I've got too many 'number one' priorities and I haven't had any decent feedback in about eight months. And I don't care whether he implies I'm ineffectual for asking for this help. As far as I am concerned it says more about him than it does about me.

2. I'm going to decide each day, each week, each month the priorities for the next day or week or month. I'm fed up with getting embroiled in trivia.

3. I'm going to take a day off to get my filing system sorted.

Unplugged Principle 2: the principle of wisdom

• What skills would be directly helpful to you? <u>Write them down</u>.

• What skills would be not so obvious, but great fun anyway? <u>Write them down</u>.

• How much time are you investing in developing your brain per month? <u>Write it down</u>.

• How much money are you investing in developing your brain per month? <u>Write it down</u>.

- Whose wisdom do you respect? <u>Write their names down</u>.
- Reflect back five years. How much wiser are you now? <u>Write it down</u>.
- Project forward five years. How much wiser will you have become? In what way? <u>Write it down</u>.

Now, pause for a few minutes. Read all of your answers. Again, put pen to paper or fingers to keyboard and write as quickly as you can the continuation to this statement:

I can restore wisdom to my work by carrying out the following three actions:

1. _____

2. _____

3. _____

Example

I can restore wisdom to my work by carrying out the following three actions:

1. I will go to HR and find out what courses are available to me/what training budget is allocated to me and get onto every course I can.
2. I will buy one highly recommended business book and read it, even if it takes me one year to do so.
3. I will teach myself how to juggle three balls.

Unplugged Principle 3: the principle of passion

- What could you give more 'oomph' to? <u>Write it down.</u>
- What is the intrinsic worth of some of those essential tasks? <u>Write it down.</u>
- Who/what drains your passion? <u>Write it down.</u>
- Who/what motivates you at work? <u>Write it down.</u>

Now, pause for a few minutes. Read all of your answers. Again, put pen to paper or fingers to keyboard and write as quickly as you can the continuation to this statement:

I can restore passion to my work by carrying out the following three actions:

1. _____

2. _____

3. _____

<u>Example</u>

I can restore passion to my work by carrying out the following three actions:

1. Choosing my response and choosing the response of enthusiasm.
2. Looking after myself: taking my breaks.
3. Simply having the belief that whatever project I get it is excellent development for me and I will do it to the best of my ability.

Unplugged Principle 4: the principle of direction

- This week, this month, this year: what are you trying to achieve? <u>Write it down</u>.
- In what are you investing? Consider product, people, purpose, clarification. <u>Write down your responses.</u>
- What areas of your Life are most driven by urgency? <u>Write it down</u>.
- What are the causes of urgency in your Life? <u>Write it down</u>.

Now, pause for a few minutes. Read all of your answers. Again, put pen to paper or fingers to keyboard and write as quickly as you can the continuation to this statement:

I can restore direction to my work by carrying out the following three actions:

1. _____

2. _____

3. _____

<u>Example</u>

I can restore direction to my work by carrying out the following three actions:

1   Adopting the compass concept.
2. Adopting the master list concept.
3. Taking ten minutes out each day to ask (1) how am I doing? and (2) how can I get back on track?

Unplugged Principle 5: the principle of possibility

- What are you trying to control that cannot be controlled? <u>Write them down</u>?
- Are you reviewing and learning from every cock-up? <u>Give some example</u>s.
- What needs to be done but is currently blocked? <u>Make a note</u>.

Now, pause for a few minutes. Read all of your answers. Again, put pen to paper or fingers to keyboard and write as quickly as you can the continuation to this statement:

I can restore possibility to my work by carrying out the following three actions:

1. _____

2. _____

3. _____

<u>Example</u>

I can restore possibility to my work by carrying out the following three actions:

1. I will seriously focus on flip-siding, starting now.
2. I realise the difference between what I can and can't control. I will decide not to worry about that which I cannot control.
3. I will buy, read, mark-up and use a book on creativity.

Unplugged Principle 6: the principle of love

- Which relationships could you invest in? <u>Write them down</u>.
- What is your current customer service strategy? <u>How could you upgrade it to the next level?</u>
- What does love mean to you? What could it mean? <u>Write it down</u>.

Now, pause for a few minutes. Read all of your answers. Again, put pen to paper or fingers to keyboard and write as quickly as you can the continuation to this statement:

I can restore love to my work by carrying out the following three actions:

1. _____

2. _____

3. _____

<u>Example</u>

I can restore love to my work by carrying out the following three actions:

1. Noticing the value difference brings rather than being annoyed by it.
2. Encouraging more diversity of background in the recruitment process.
3. Simply 'going out' to people more.

Unplugged Principle 7: the principle of being

- Who are you? <u>Write it down</u>.
- What do you stand for? <u>Write it down</u>.
- What is your organisation? <u>Write it down</u>.
- What does your organisation stand for? <u>Write it down</u>.

Now, pause for a few minutes. Read all of your answers. Again, put pen to paper or fingers to keyboard and write as quickly as you can the continuation to this statement:

I can restore being to my work by carrying out the following three actions:

1. _____

2. _____

3. _____

<u>Example</u>

I can restore being to my work by carrying out the following three actions:

1. Deciding to carry out the behaviours of the person I want to become.
2. Working as much on my thinking as my actions
3. Taking time out simply to 'be'.

LIVING *UNPLUGGED*: AT HOME

Many of us would prefer that our home were our sanctuary: our place of rest, of recuperation, of thinking, of hospitality. Instead, it often becomes a battleground: a place of tension, a place of argument, a place of business.

Follow these discussion points to restore *unplugged* thinking to your home. If you are in a close relationship with someone, then involve them in your thinking, too.

***Unplugged* Principle 1: the principle of simplicity**

Consider

- What stuff, what things can you get rid of?
  - The pasta-making machine?
  - The old baby stuff?
  - Your books from college/university?
  - Music you will never listen to again?
  - Printers, toasters and paintbrushes which you no longer need?
  - The old gardening clothes you no longer need?
  - The 'just in case' stuff?
- How quickly could you:
  - Clear the attic?
  - Clear the garage?

- Clear the cupboards under the sink in the kitchen?
- Deliver those unwanted books to charity shops?
- Sell those CDs on eBay?
- What ideas can you get rid of?
  - That complicated is clever.
  - That complicated is better.
  - That complicated is sophisticated.
  - That simple is simplistic.
- By when could you
  - Write down the names of the five most important people in your life?
  - Write down the names of the three most important things in your life?
  - The day and hour on which you will fully implement this principle?
- What ideas can you restore/take on board?
  - Simple is simple.
  - Simple is empowering
  - Simple is enlivening
  - Simple would restore what is close to your heart.
  - It used to be simple, it could be simple again.
  - Anything can be simple.
    - Child-rearing.
    - The new product launch.
    - My commute.
    - The start-up.

- My return to health.
- What is stopping you?
  - Starting? Simply START NOW!
  - Help? Who or what could help you?
  - Worry? Stop worrying and start doing!

***Unplugged* Principle 2: the principle of wisdom**

Consider

- How can you invest in yourself?
  - What courses can you go on?
  - What's your personal investment budget?
  - What's your best medium for learning?
    - CD?
    - Book?
    - Class?
    - Experiment?
    - 1:1 coaching?
- Who do you admire?
  - For what do you admire them?
  - What values and beliefs do they have and hold?
  - Where could you learn more about them?
  - What have been the great learnings of your Life so far?

- Of what do you regularly need to remind yourself?
  - To invest in you.
  - To take time out.
  - To look after yourself.
  - To do less to achieve more.
- How could you keep this happening?
  - Set up a learning team?
  - Get a mentor?
  - Book on a course at college?
- What are you currently
  - Reading?
  - Listening to in the car?
  - Thinking about and discussing?

Unplugged Principle 3: the principle of passion

Consider

- What happened to your enthusiasm?
  - What at times can block it?
  - What at times can frustrate you?
  - What at times can cause deep fatigue?
- What makes you enthusiastic?
  - What are your best times (and don't just reply 'holidays'!)

- What is enthusiasm to you?
  - What does it look like?
  - What does it feel like?
  - What does it sound like?
- In what activities will you look for more intrinsic worth?
  - Looking after the children?
  - Helping around the house?
  - Community affairs?
  - Your partner's work/interests?
- Where and when will you practise the approaches of
  - Flip-siding?
  - Intrinsic worth?
  - State management?
- What would passion look like
  - At a team meeting?
  - At the kid's birthday party?

Unplugged Principle 4: the principle of direction

Consider

- Where are you going?
  - In your career?
  - Now?

- In the future?
- Is that what you want?
- With your mind/body:
  - What state is it in now?
  - What state do you want it to be in?
- With your personal finances:
  - What are the two major changes you need to make?
- With your relationships:
  - Which is THE one you need to work on?
- In having fun?
- In ensuring your contribution to the bigger picture?
  - How will you get there?
- Do you have a buddy?
- Reading or a course, maybe?
- What 'time management' practices will you:
  - Ditch for ever?
  - Adopt?
- Personal compass monthly review?
- Daily master list management?

Unplugged Principle 5: the principle of possibility

Consider

- What are you trying to control that cannot be controlled?
  - The moods of your partner?
  - The worries of your teenage son?
  - The weather at the weekend?
- What are you not managing that you could do?
  - Your response to your partner, your son?
- In what can you become more of a possibility thinker?
  - Your business activity?
  - Your finances?
  - Your career?
- Are you ready for regular inspiration on the topics of
  - Creativity?
  - Intuition?
  - Possibility?
  - Meaningful coincidences?
- How would you handle these big questions?
  - If you knew money was not an issue, what would you do?
  - If you knew you couldn't fail, what would you do?

Unplugged Principle 6: the principle of love

Consider

- Who do you love?
  - How do you show them that you love them?
  - Do they know how much you love them?
- Who could you love more?
- What worries you about the word 'love'?
- What do you expect in return for 'love'?
- What is love for
  - A lover?
  - A friend?
  - A customer?

Unplugged Principle 7: the principle of being

Consider

- Who are you?
  - What label did you give to yourself?
  - Ask yourself again: who are you?
- Who do you want to become?
- For who you want to become, what might you be doing?

- What can you do more of on a day-to-day basis?
  - Be here now: not forever capturing your life on film?
  - Taking time out?
  - Learning to be?

LIVING *UNPLUGGED*: FOR THE KIDS

Children benefit hugely from living *unplugged*. It's their natural *modus operandi*. They love freedom. They love knowing and exploring. They thrive on receiving unconditional love. We have mistakenly over the last twenty years surely, definitely, and with increasing speed, removed their childhood. We have encouraged them to plug in at every opportunity (TV in every room, computing power everywhere, mobile ever to hand) and we have plugged them in as often as we can (to busy schedules, to apparent security via lifts to school, to 'on-line' capabilities). They act grown up but we have not allowed them to do so: to actually 'grow up'. Consequently, many remain immature, lacking the ability to take personal responsibility, to reflect, but above all to be truly happy. Encouraging and allowing them to live *unplugged* will restore an appropriate childhood to them, will allow them to mature, will allow them to realise their talents and above all be happy.

We are in danger as a society of removing this potential to live such an *unplugged* life from our children. We have handed our own understandable but grossly exaggerated fears of the world to them. We have endowed them with a screen-based and consequently trance-inducing world.

Break out and encourage them to live and think *unplugged*.

Here are some suggested points for you to ponder. If there are two of you bringing up the children, use it as a discussion point. If you are on your own, buddy up with another enlightened parent. As your children get a little older, encourage them to think about such points themselves.

Unplugged Principle 1: the principle of simplicity

FOR YOU and YOUR PARTNER to CONSIDER

- What do you want for your children? What are the most important gifts you would wish for them? Make it really simple. Can you say it in a word or two?
- What values, such as the value of simplicity, do you wish to instil?
- How could you make your children's lives simpler, more straightforward? Remember that simple does not equal boring, nor simplistic. Simple is empowering, just as too much complexity is debilitating.
- What straightforward routines and processes would make life easier for them?
- What exhausts your children? What causes them unnecessary anxiety?
- What do you simply need to say NO to in their life?

Example

You and your partner do a quick analysis of how your two children, aged 4 and 6, spend their time each week. You are shocked to discover that nearly every minute of their week is a pre-arranged (e.g. music club) or default (e.g. watching a Disney DVD) activity. You decide to create 'empty time'. Empty time is when nothing is pre-arranged. There may initially be battles over 'why can't we have a video?' or 'please take us to the park', but <u>no</u>. You do of course stay loving, but you leave them to it: this is a period of thinking for themselves. If nothing else they could sit and read (shock horror!).

FOR YOU to DISCUSS with YOUNG CHILDREN

• The value of simplicity. Relate to great stories: the recurrence of the simple parables; good versus evil; the value of the wait; true beauty. As you read to them and as you encourage them to read, remind them that the great messages are all simple. And powerful.
• Give them simple responsibilities from the earliest age: carrying in the groceries from the car and stacking it away for you. Making their own bed. Putting the books back in the book-box.

Example

You and your partner identify five values which you would like your children to practise, e.g. integrity, loyalty, valuing simplicity, and read them stories which support those simple values.

FOR YOU to DISCUSS with YOUNG ADULTS

- What is really important to them? How can they get back on track for those?
- What are their values? How can they live those?
- Encourage them to discuss their thoughts and concerns; in particular, encourage them to 'teach back' to you in a simple way.

Example

You and your partner decide to own a couple of each of the subjects your children are studying and support through 'teach-back', quizzing and helping find interesting material. For example, one of your children is studying World War II for GCSE. Go for a walk and have a discussion on topics such as why are many of us now appalled by the bombing on Dresden but it seemed right at the time? Was it right at the time but wrong with hindsight? These are not topics which are too difficult. You'll be amazed what your children can get to grips with. And if they can get their head around them think how they'll avoid the generalisations of many people's thinking.

Unplugged Principle 2: the principle of wisdom

FOR YOU and YOUR PARTNER to CONSIDER

- How can you help your children value wisdom over 'stuff'?
- What can you do to ensure there is a sense and a value of learning in the house?
- What is the relative value given to screen vs. book? To celebrity vs. philosopher? To clarity of thought vs. 'dunno/whatever'.
- How do you tackle 'this is boring', 'I hate maths', 'I'm no good at maths'.
- Why not ensure a proportion of their pocket money is dedicated for books?

Example

You and your partner make an agreement to be careful in your own discussion in front of the children as to what you attach apparent priorities; you decide to consciously ensure there is a balance and it's not just 'how exciting it would be to get a big screen TV', but also 'Saturday is visit the library day'.

FOR YOU to DISCUSS with YOUNG CHILDREN

- How can we look at this another way to make it interesting?
- No, you may not be as good as Picasso, however …
- How about if you learnt it properly rather than just for the test tomorrow?

Example

When discussing points with the children, look for the deeper point beyond just the 'wow' factor.

Yes – Newton 'discovered' gravity, but <u>observation</u> was key.

Yes – Nelson was a tremendous leader, but his <u>care</u> for his men was vital.

Yes – grandma was a gardener, but her <u>patience</u> was essential.

FOR YOU to DISCUSS with YOUNG ADULTS

- Who do you admire? What expertise do they have? What is their talent?
- What is your talent?
- The nature/nurture debate.

Example

An important discussion to have with young adults as they go through that challenging stage of coping with a rapidly developing body and a changing way of thinking is 'what will take them to where they want to be?' Sure they have some talents, but they need wisdom to release that talent.

Unplugged Principle 3: the principle of passion

FOR YOU and YOUR PARTNER to CONSIDER

- What role modelling of enthusiasm do you provide?
- The value of being bored, but not accepting 'boring'.
- The difference between passion and personality.

Example

Neither you nor your partner need to be superheroes, but consider whether your children hear you whinging and complaining, or focusing on what is working well and how to be resourceful.

FOR YOU to DISCUSS with YOUNG CHILDREN

- Beginning to think about choosing their response to a situation.
- The simple concepts of being 'cheerful', 'resourceful' and 'helpful', especially when they haven't been asked.

Example

Even the youngest children can begin to learn and need to learn that not everything can always go their way. That is Life. Teach them flip-siding. Show them that you flip-side and that a sense of humour can go a long way.

FOR YOU to DISCUSS with YOUNG ADULTS

- That attitude will have a huge factor in their ability to learn.

- And in their employability.

- That you can't always change what is happening to you, but you can change your attitude.

<u>Example</u>

Remind and encourage them to realise that attitude is always a choice. And that is fantastic because it can overlay any talent ability that they might have. It is particularly important for young children that their Life is not too sanitised, that they do begin to understand about death, about war, about human prejudice and unpleasantness.

Unplugged Principle 4: the principle of direction

FOR YOU and YOUR PARTNER to CONSIDER

- Help your children to consider their direction: what is important to them in the future?

- Encourage them to think about other aspects as well as just money or fame. Be careful about suggesting that they are mutually exclusive, e.g. that for happiness you need to be poor, or that you cannot be happy if you have wealth.

- Education. Encourage your children to think about this broadly (i.e. beyond just the school remit). In particular, getting them to follow what they truly want.

Example

Are you a good example? Do you talk about being trapped? Or do you see the possibilities of where you are?

Does an element of risk come with your job; are you paid by results? Could you be fired if you do not perform? And are the children aware of that? How do they view that?

How do you view security? Are you chasing it? Can you really get it?

FOR YOU to DISCUSS with YOUNG CHILDREN

- Support them in their dreams: do not allow their dreams to be squashed.
- Read inspirational stories.
- Show them great stories from the press.

Example

Unfortunately, even the most well-meaning of teachers can say the wrong things, often just as an aside e.g. 'you'll never be able to become a vet'. Keep in touch with what is happening at school. Talk to your kids and then such assumptions will become apparent and can be rapidly rectified.

FOR YOU to DISCUSS with YOUNG ADULTS

- Giving early experience of jobs: encourage them to take earning responsibility.
- Supporting their job applications: don't talk them out of being a journalist or whatever they seek.

Example

Battling for the dream job: acting, being a DJ or a Vet. These require courage and discipline. Instil such qualities from the earliest age .

***Unplugged* Principle 5: the principle of possibility**

FOR YOU and YOUR PARTNER to CONSIDER

- Reminding them that, despite technology and modern science, we cannot control everything.
- Work on what we can manage and control.
- Respect that which we cannot.
- We can manage our response.

Example

So are you a good example of possibility thinking? When things don't go your way are you able to manage, can you take an alternative approach? How? What do you do?

FOR YOU to DISCUSS with YOUNG CHILDREN

- No you can't have the bike at the moment: what else could you play with?
- We're not able to go to Disney for your Birthday, what else would be fun?

Example

Make sure they know their history, Being warm, comfortable, being able to get hold of food 24 by 7: these are all aspects of the very recent past and should not be taken for granted. Remind them of the delicate web/infrastructure which supports all of this. Ask them, what would they do (1) if there were no electricity for 24 hours (2) the shops were going to be shut for three days. Get them thinking and see what happens.

FOR YOU to DISCUSS with YOUNG ADULTS

• So the grade that you got in that GCSE was too low to allow you to do the AS, what can we do?

• So you didn't get the A2 grades you needed, what can we do?

<u>Example</u>

What could you do instead? Now that your girlfriend/boyfriend has dumped you? Now that you have lost the job at the café for being late?

Unplugged Principle 6: the principle of love

FOR YOU and YOUR PARTNER to CONSIDER

• What is love for each of you?

• What would be unconditional love for your children?

• What will enhance a more sensitive, caring approach in your children?

• Distinguishing between love and sex. What are your needs in both areas?

<u>Example</u>

How do you demonstrate love? Hugs, kisses, supportive talk. Little things. Remembering what is important in your partner's Life? Some rituals (a favourite meal). Some spontaneity.

FOR YOU to DISCUSS with YOUNG CHILDREN

• What do you mean by love, by friendship, by sex?

The biggest one is of course trying to get some balance with this topic of sex. SEX SEX SEX. OK, but what else? Is there anything else?

<u>Example</u>

FOR YOU to DISCUSS with YOUNG ADULTS

• What is the difference and the connection between love and sex?

<u>Example</u>

More of the same. What makes for long-term sustainable relationships?

Unplugged Principle 7: the principle of being

FOR YOU and YOUR PARTNER to CONSIDER

What would it mean for you to be

• 'authentic'?

• 'real'?

• 'self/internally-referenced'?

• What would it take/what would need to be different for these to happen for you?

<u>Example</u>

Are you honest with your partner? Not rude, nor direct. But do you talk about what is really important to each other? Do you express concerns: concerns in general, about the children, about each other? And with the latter, not necessarily expecting change but simply allowing the point to be expressed.

FOR YOU to DISCUSS with YOUNG CHILDREN

What sort of person do they want to be? Funny? Caring? Curious? How can they develop their being?

Example

Really notice. <u>Really</u> notice how different each of your children are. Don't put them on a conveyor belt. Don't expect them to be like you. They may or may not like camping or classical music or cookery or football or ballet .

Lucy wants to be a vet. Great, but what is it about being a vet which appeals?

FOR YOU to DISCUSS with YOUNG ADULTS

- Who are they now and who do they want to become?
- The concept of acting as the person they wish to become?

Example

Tim wants to become a police officer. If he were a police officer now, how would he behave in that situation?

LIVING *UNPLUGGED*: THE GUIDELINES SUMMARISED

Here in one section is a complete list of the *Unplugged* principles, each with their ten implementation guidelines. Use these as a guide as you begin to live and breathe each of the principles.

Work on them as you wish; some possibilities are:

- Each day choose a number from one to seven and then a number from one to ten. Choose each number at random. The number from one to seven is the *unplugged* principle to work on. The number from one to ten is which guideline to consider.
- Set up a learning team (three people who meet for one hour each month to support each other's learning). Choose one principle that you will each work on for that month and report back successes and findings.
- Coach someone (in your family or in your team) to use one of the principles.
- Create your own simple summary card of the principles which you can carry with you and refer to occasionally.

Unplugged Principle 1: the principle of simplicity

Simplicity 1 Ask: what do you really want with your Life? Ask: what do we really want here? What is most important about my career? What is most important about the children's schooling? What do I personally want for my Life? *This is the 'red light (STOP & think!)' question.*

Simplicity 2 Decide. Decide to adopt an *unplugged* lifestyle, where simplicity has greater value to you than complexity, from food to relationships. Work on it as a team/family. At your family meeting (see bonus 1), regularly ask how could we make things simpler? Whenever you are about to take something on, consider questions such as:

- *To take this on, what am I going to drop?* E.g. if I sign up at the gym, that's going to mean two evenings per week and much of Sunday morning. What will I drop? Well, certainly I'll drop staying late at the office; that's partly the point of this change. On Sunday morning, I'll replace the time which used to be for reading the newspapers which to be honest are no big deal and I think I'm actually a bit addicted to and I'll be glad to work at that addiction, once and for all.

- *By taking this on how will it makes things simpler overall?* E.g. this new routine will: get me fitter, break the pattern of staying late, break the pattern of being addicted to the newspapers.

This is the 'unplug' action.

Simplicity 3 Decide to enjoy fewer things really well rather than try to do a lot of things badly. Films, books, relationships, meals; all become more enjoyable if they are not rushed or fitted in between other activities. Think quantity times quality; keep the quantity to a manageable number and then decide to concentrate on quality. Decide to focus on quality rather than society's fundamental – mistaken – mantra of 'more'.

This is the 'less is more' action.

Simplicity 4 Work at those fewer things so that you move through the simplistic (the 'this is hard, what's the point?' stage) to the complex ('this is very hard, this requires a lot of attention, this is becoming too much' stage) to simplicity ('this is straightforward, this is a no-brainer. I can do this without thinking about it; truly straightforward ...' stage) This is true of the gym, it is true of a relationship ... It is true of anything which is worthwhile, in fact.

This is the 'simplicity beyond complexity' action.

Simplicity 5 Reduce data input: you can do it. All that stuff filling up your brain. When stuff is filling your brain then you are not able to get the best ideas out. Stop it. Papers, magazines, TV watching hours, Sunday Papers. Get serious about data deprivation.

- Get off mailing lists: return all junk mail with a request to be taken off the list.
- Reduce unwanted phone-calls: get ex-directory.
- Reduce junk e-mails and texts: use the blockers which your software provides.
- Cancel the Sunday Papers: go on, you can do it.
- Switch the TV off: again, you can do it.

This is the 'data deprivation' action.

Simplicity 6 Don't try and keep up with the Joneses. Decide now that you will decide your lifestyle and it will be driven primarily by the quality of Life that you are seeking. When you change your lifestyle you will not be affected by what others say or how they think. There are some things which are very important to you and you will do those properly, never minding the comments of others.

This is the 'quality of life' action.

Simplicity 7 Create chunks of time in your diary to do the activities that are important to you: don't micro schedule. Make those chunks sensible lengths. Remember we work best when we get involved in a subject. Too much chopping and changing is debilitating. At work and home for shorter time-scale activities, practise batching them; do half-an-hour's sorting out of the finances and bill paying, for instance.

This is the 'whose life?' Question.

Simplicity 8 Decide the ten most important things in your Life now and make them happen: create a simplicity jar, get those smooth rocks and a clear jar. Write on each of those stones with felt pen what is important to you. Remember that if you fill up the jar with the sand and little pebbles of wasteful activity, you will never fit your rocks into the jar. Get them in first, and then see how much room is left.

This is the 'rocks in the jar' action.

Simplicity 9 When purchasing products and committing to services, don't be 'sold-up', don't get stuff that you don't really need. Buy the simplest microwave that'll do the job, don't be feature seduced. Do not even think about buying a fresh pasta-making machine unless authentic Italian cooking is your absolute love. Demand simplicity from your professional advisers. Yes, but what does a 'bond' really mean?

This is the 'low feature' action.

Simplicity 10 Simplicity audit. Regularly carry out a simplicity audit. Ask:

i.   What is bugging me/us?

ii.   What is taking up unnecessary time?

iii. What causes the arguments in this household/this business?

iv. What are the frustrations, the frankly tedious?

v.   Where do we waste money?

vi.   What things do we do that cause problems down the line?

This is the 'spring clean' question.

In everything we do, we seek simplicity. We avoid making things unnecessarily complex. We realise that simplicity is a very special case beyond complexity.

Unplugged Principle 2: the principle of wisdom

Mind 1 Decide to invest in your brain. Switch your emphasis from investment in stuff to investment in brain. Invest at least as much in your brain as you do in your car. At the very least go for 2% of your income. In particular, decide to develop your reflective intelligence, the intelligence which comes from simply stopping and thinking. Use it!

This is the 'invest' action.

Mind 2 Read more. More books and also more widely. Books are unique in that they allow you to pause, consider and reflect. They allow you to engage with the ideas. They offer a far more powerful learning medium than TV. Decide a personal budget on non-fiction books; start with say £10.00 per month. Yes you can afford it.

This is the 'read' action.

Mind 3 Discuss and talk: over meals or while walking. Practise appreciating other ideas. Different ideas and ideas of people you don't like. Allow ideas to be explored without a definite answer having to be formed. Practise philosophy. Maybe book a course.

This is the 'discuss' action.

Mind 4 Allow some data deprivation time so that your brain can utilise all of those great ideas.
By data deprivation we mean:
i.   quiet times: no radio/TV nor music
ii. no newspaper/reading
iii. a meditation
iv. a walk

This is the 'data deprivation' action.

Mind 5 Develop your brain (1): Practise giving attention to enable you to get the results that you seek.

Nothing happens without <u>attention</u>. Family life/business life/personal life tend to move towards complexity because we fail to give attention to a fundamental Law of the Universe and that is that things tend to move to a state of increasing disorder unless we decide to reverse the process: we reverse the process by giving attention.

Attention is dedicated focus. When we give someone or something attention, it begins to cause change. If we give our garden attention such as doing some weeding, doing some pruning, adjusting the beds a little, it becomes more attractive. If we give our bank account some attention, tracking where the money is going, it rapidly begins to improve. Attention is the primary function of choice. To become more attentive:

- Look after your state.
- Practise holding attention on something until it changes as you seek.
- Practise making a conscious choice rather than simply reacting.

This is the 'give attention' action.

Mind 6 Develop your brain (2): practise creativity to enable you to quickly solve problems.
By creativity we mean thinking outside the normal standard patterns. Creativity is the recognition of alternative choices. Creativity is breaking a pattern. To become more creative:

- Practise looking at the problem in alternate ways
- Develop your creativity tools
- Think outside the box.
- Break the pattern.
- Realise that the way you are looking at the problem may well be the problem.

This is the 'create' action.

Mind 7 Develop your brain(3): encourage and use your intuition in order to see connections and possibilities. Realise this is a valid way of looking at things: you do not need to ignore ideas generated in this way simply because they do not seem logical. Intuition is the noticing of what is happening, it is re-sensitising to both what is happening around (for input) and what is happening within you (for guidance). To develop your intuition:

- Slow down so that you are more sensitive.
- Listen and notice your inner guidance, in particular heart and gut.
- Consider: 'why have I decided that mind thinking is more valid than heart/gut feeling?'

This is the 'intuit' action.

Mind 8 Develop your brain (4): allow synchronicity to become a part of your Life so that the universe supports you a little more and then a lot more. Once flow state is working for us we will begin to notice occurrences of synchronicity. This is where the universe begins to work on our behalf. ***We tell our partner one evening about an old friend we've long lost contact with, and how much that friendship meant to us – the next day we bump into him in Starbucks. Many people will dismiss this as coincidence. Well maybe it is, but we notice these coincidences, or synchronistic events, because they have some meaning for us. If, instead of ignoring or dismissing them, we pay attention to their meaning and look for what benefits can come out of them, we open ourselves to all sorts of possibilities that otherwise might just pass us by***.

This is the 'notice synchronicity' action.

Mind 9 Develop your luck by networking and 'right effort'. By networking we mean going out to people, by helping them out so that they are likely to help you out. By 'right effort' we mean considering people as much as the task. Networking is using the power of our thinking to go out and connect with others. Why? For fun, for their development and for our benefit. Networking is just giving a little more focus (see bonus 1) when we meet and work with people. How can we help them? How can they help us? Importantly when we make maximum use of networking we are clear on our personal brand (see bonus 10). Keep your network safe: database or excel or word or a pile of 3 by 5 cards; whatever works for you.

This is the 'develop luck' action.

Mind 10 Decide to be internally referenced and think for yourself. To do this, establish your values and principles. Then stick to those and decide not to be swayed by the views of others.

This is the 'be self-referenced' action.

Unplugged Principle 3: the principle of passion

Passion 1 Ensure your fundamental mantra is: whatever you do, do it with passion. Each moment is a choice: choose passion.

Passion 2 Be here now. Whatever is happening, stay grounded. Be where you are. Be here now.

Passion 3 Be clear on your vision: when you have a clear *want* and *why* that puts fear and lethargy in its place. Make that vision absolutely clear, absolutely focused.

Passion 4 Have a fair expectation of Life: no one said it was going to be or was meant to be easy. But Life being hard does not mean it need not be enjoyable.

Passion 5 Nurture yourself so that you are brimming with energy: invest with time for you, take sensible exercise.

Passion 6 Take care with language such as
   a.   I have to do it. Check out *why*. Why do I have to do it? Ask yourself, what would happen if I didn't do it?
   b.   I ought to do it. Check out *why*. Why ought I to do it? What would happen if I didn't?
   c.   I should do it. Check out *why*. Why should I do it? What would happen?

Passion 7 Manage fear and uncertainty: three useful mind-sets:
   d.   No failure only feedback: whatever happens, decide to learn from it.
   e.   The past is history; I can design the future; forget the past if it is no longer helpful.
   f.   Uncertainty reveals my greatest opportunities; it has in the past and it will do in the future.

Passion 8 Look for the intrinsic worth in whatever you do. Dig deep. What experience will you gain? How will you help someone?

Passion 9 Flip-side if necessary. There will always be something we can get from any experience. Simply look for the possibility, whatever it might be.

Passion 10 The quest for happiness does not mean there will not be pain or anguish on the path. But the pain, the anguish, even the depression is part of the route to long/longer term happiness.

Unplugged **Principle 4: the principle of direction**

Direction 1 Decide to set your personal direction, to set your compass. On your personal compass there are six compass points:

i.   Career.
ii. Mind/body.
iii. Finance.
iv. Relationships.
v.   Fun.
vi. Contribution.

Direction 2 Manage each of the six compass points via your Master List.

A typical 'to do' list is based only on what is urgent, short term and often 'quick-fix'. Ditch the 'to do'; sit and work your compass actions. After a short transition period you will notice that the urgency will begin to drop away.

Direction 3 Create momentum through 'break and date'. The challenge with a master list is that it contains the big stuff, the fundamental stuff. Although exciting, it is often daunting. How on earth do I get this done? How do I break this down? What will make this happen? The answer is to break it down into smaller components and do that again if necessary until it becomes time – and brain – friendly.

Direction 4 Create perspective: Take regular breaks to consider your direction. Ten minutes every day to plan your diary, 30 minutes every week to make sure that you know what the important, investing actions are for you that week. Every month put aside an hour to focus on your direction, where you want to go next, how you are doing so far. And twice a year, take half a day as a retreat to assess your life and once again ask the important question, 'What is important to me?'

Direction 5 Stretch your horizon: what do you want to be doing a week from now? A month? A year? Three years? Five years?

Direction 6 Read for inspiration which keeps you focused on your direction: 'no one on their deathbed ever said I should have spent more time at the office ...'

Direction 7 Establish a direction indicator. Draw your vision: stick it above your desk, stick it on the fridge. Look at it every day.

Direction 8 Ensure you take regular breaks to deliberately break the addictive nature of urgency. Learn how to manage your breathing at times of stress.

Direction 9 Work on your state so that you have an inclination to act and choose, rather than become addicted to the thrill and/or fear of urgency.

Direction 10 Decide that you will start now, following your direction now.

Unplugged Principle 5: the principle of possibility

Possibility 1 Pay attention to chaotic systems. Step 1 is to become chaos systems literate.

To do this start noticing chaotic systems, start working with them, start using them.

Here are some notable chaotic systems which you may not have 'noticed' before:

- Market forces
- Team dynamics
- Your health
- Your career
- The stock market.

Apart from of course the weather, perhaps the most famous of chaotic systems.

Possibility 2 Seek the patterns that emerge from such systems; use those as best you can.

For example:

- Your local weather. If you give it attention, you will begin to notice patterns: cloud formations, sky colours. None of this will guarantee that you can tell what the weather is going to be like, but it's probably more accurate than the local weather forecast.
- Team dynamics. There's no way you can accurately predict exactly what is going to happen. But with sensitivity, careful observation and attention, you can begin to notice trends.
- Your health. Again, you cannot accurately predict your health. But after a while you notice that your ear is feeling a little hot and this, and this ...

Possibility 3 Be aware that 'easy order' is only a very special case that we happen to find attractive because it allows such predictability. Remember in maths when the stuff you did always turned out to be a 'special case'? Remember in French that the most commonly used verbs are all irregular? Remember in science that atoms are not hard billiard-ball like objects? Interesting that, isn't it? Remember that the edge of all subjects is easy, predictable. But the depth, the inside of all subjects is chaotic, mysterious ...

Possibility 4 Chaotic systems rather than simple systems will become the new norm. For a variety of reasons but certainly including the fact that we are a small world now, it is likely that chaotic systems will continue to impact our day-to-day existence.

Possibility 5 Have you noticed how when you have really struggled with something, really worked your way through the mess, and the chaos, you arrive at an elegant understanding? That is the definitive, the ultimate intelligence. From such definitive intelligence are derived the true principles of freedom and success.

Possibility 6 Do not attempt to stamp out chaos; work at it step by step, whether it is the challenge of getting fit again, whether it is the challenge of repairing the relationship, try simply to begin the process.

Possibility 7 Finally, for ever more, never again, realise that 'absolutes' does not mean that we have gained security.

Possibility 8 Whatever happens in our quest to become more used to the world of chaos, uncertainty and possibility, remember that there is no failure, only feedback.

Possibility 9 Remember that as George Leonard (author of Mastery) so elegantly puts it, in our quest to gain mastery we must love the dip, love the plateau.

Possibility 10 Remember that chaos is the new order. Grey is the new black.

Unplugged Principle 6: the principle of love

Love 1 Re-realise that love is the most powerful force in the universe. Love influences people, grows people, kills people, makes people well, makes people sick. Love bonds nations, love bonds people. Love pulls nations apart. Decide to be more aware of how you use love as a force in your Life.

Love 2 Love is a creator, a healer, and a 'happiness instiller'. When we love someone, we influence their body chemistry for the positive. They feel better, they are nurtured. Become a healer.

Love 3 Love is the definitive business force: for the customer, for the individual. When we use love as a force in business, we are talking about the highest level of so-called 'customer service'. When you love your customer you can do no more for them.

Love 4 Be you. When you are loving, you are clearly able to love yourself. When you are ABLE to love yourself, you are able to be yourself. And when you are able to be yourself you will have no problems loving. And when you have no difficulty loving then you have no problem living.

Love 5 Be honest. When you are truly loving you are being straightforward and honest. Develop the clarity of looking straight in the eye and talking one to one. Develop the ability to be assertive.

Love 6 Go out to people. Fear has been instilled in people; it is safe to go out to people. You will feel great. Your sensitivity will grow so much that you will recognise the occasions when it is not appropriate to go out fully to some one because they have not fully developed their own emotional maturity. But do remember that by stepping out a bit, you will of course grow them.

Love 7 Value difference: one of the biggest blockers to love is the ability to accept and not judge. Try putting your energy into that: accepting and non-judging before putting someone 'in a box'.

Love 8 Love you first. Accept all that you are and all that you might become if you give yourself an opportunity.

Love 9 Don't be a super-hero; this is not about losing real human emotions. You will feel anger, resentment, annoyance, despair when trying to be more loving. But that's OK. All of those emotions are there for a reason.

Love 10 Think about:

- 'Is it better to be loving or to be right?' Anon.
- 'You cannot know someone at the same time in the light of love and the light of justice.' Niels Bohr.

Unplugged **Principle 7: the principle of being**

Being 1 Who are you? Take an A4 sheet of paper or decide to put fingers to keyboard. Head the page/screen 'Who am I?' Below that, number 25 lines. Now write on every line. Start each line with: 'I am ...' Keep doing this and keep writing. Do not stop until you get to the bottom of the page. What happened? Who are you? WHO are you? Who ARE you? Who are YOU. Silly? Perhaps. But who are you?

Being 2 Start saying 'I can!' Stop saying 'I can't'. It is true that there are some things that you physically cannot do e.g. jump off a high building and expect to survive. But there are a surprisingly large number of things that you can do: improve your memory, improve your relationship, get a better job, earn more money, solve your health problem. But the first thing you must do is to say 'I can'. Because in this context when you say 'I can't' you mean 'I choose not to'. And do you really? Become an 'I can' person.

Being 3 Remove labels. Do not define yourself by what you do. Nor by your job title nor your age nor sex, nor history. Define yourself by who you are. You may not yet run your own business, but you are an entrepreneur. You may be 55 but you have the enthusiasm (in some cases more enthusiasm) than a twenty-five year old. Drop the label; emphasise the quality.

Being 4 According to whom? Take care with should/must/ought. You should? You must? You ought? According to whom? What would happen if you did/didn't? You must go to University! Why? Because everybody else does? You ought to be more political at work. Oh? What will happen if I am not? Language is a programmer of your brain. Check that you use language which will programme it effectively.

Being 5 Check your beliefs. Remind yourself that your mindset drives your behaviour which in turn dictates your actions. If you believe that you can then you will behave in such a way and then your results are more likely to be the ones you desire and that will tend to reinforce the belief that you originally had and ... See bonus section for seven empowering beliefs.

Being 6 Get into flow state. Experience flow state more often: a state in which you simply are who you want to be. You are that writer, so your writing happens. You <u>are</u> a carpenter so your wood-working begins to happen. With flow state we withhold judgement of our abilities, we accept our strengths and talents, we get on with it, we have no sense of time. And amazingly we produce, but without overly doing, more by 'being'.

Being 7 Think entrepreneur: build your brand. There are brands which excite. There are brands which are dull. Those which excite have spirit, have soul. Decide to build your personal brand to be the latter. For help on building your brand, see bonus section.

Being 8 Undertake 'being' practice. Undertake practices which 'restore the spirit', which allow you to be who you are more fully, more regularly, more steadily, more consistently. What are these practices? As simple and as varied as walking the dog, taking a walk, fishing, tai chi meditation. For a simple breathing meditation, see bonus section.

Being 9 Accepting more and judging less. Practise more acceptance, fewer judgements.

Being 10 Notice connections, consequences and critical path. Open your eyes, notice what is happening around you. Notice the impact that you have on people. Notice that who you are has a greater impact on people than what you do. Realise that everything you do has a consequence down the line.

LIVING *UNPLUGGED*: FOR LIFE

To become *unplugged* is to become authentic, to get back to the 'real you'. The 'real you' that you lost amongst the scrabbling of day-to-day living. The real you that you lost as a consequence of being seduced by the nonsense of the lifestyle merchants. To become 'unplugged' means that you no longer are propped up by a series of distracting support systems, no longer is each day such a struggle, no longer are you wondering 'what the heck is this all about?' Hey, there are plenty of challenges but you take these in your stride and realise that in fact they are not to be avoided. They are just Life. No one said Life was meant to be <u>easy</u>. Life is the definitive personal development programme: it's free as it comes bundled with you, it's always on and there is abundant feedback if you care to take it. You have energy and passion about what you need to do. And even when you cannot choose what you want to do, you can choose how you respond to what it is you need to do.

It seems an obvious thing to do, so why don't more people return to their *unplugged* state?

There is a simple answer and that is fear. Fear. But fear of what?
Fear of what people will think.
Fear of where it might take you.
Fear of whether it will really work.

These fears are all valid.

We would never want to get rid of fear. But importantly, fear is not necessarily saying don't do something. It is simply saying consider this carefully, which you would want to do anyway.

The fear of what people will think is asking you to consider whether you really wish to be different from many others? I have no doubt that you do.

The fear of where it may take you is reminding you to consider that this will probably create a whole new you. And not everybody will like it! Why not? They think they'll lose you (actually they're gaining the real you) and they realise how they could also create the change they seek. But whatever, I think you're up for it. Respect the views of others, be sensitive to their concerns, but stick with it.

The fear of whether it will really work is reminding you that this won't necessarily be easy: there may be some set-backs. But you can manage those for the bigger picture. Go for it.

When you decide to become *unplugged*, you will be tested by fear. You will be working against the crowd so much of the time. The crowd who chase things in the hope of happiness, the crowd who jam more into their days for fear of being left behind, the crowd who deride learning and thinking, the crowd for whom love is just a temporary state of infatuation, the crowd for whom 'being' is too much of a 'new-age' sound-bite. But that fear will soon settle as you enjoy the benefits of living unplugged. Of feeling engaged again, of feeling passionate and happy once more, of feeling valuable and stimulated and fearless.

Decide to work, play, live and love *unplugged*. Go on!